A FATHER'S PLACE

Mary Pytches

HODDER AND STOUGHTON
LONDON   SYDNEY   AUCKLAND

British Library Cataloguing in Publication Data

A catalogue record for this title
is available from the British Library

ISBN 0-340-60020-9

Published by Hodder and Stoughton,
a division of Hodder and Stoughton Ltd,
Mill Road, Dunton Green, Sevenoaks, Kent TN13 2YA
Editorial Office: 47 Bedford Square, London WC1B 3DP

Typeset by Hewer Text Composition Services, Edinburgh
Printed in Great Britain by Cox & Wyman Ltd, Reading, Berks

Contents

INTRODUCTION

While writing this book, I attended a youth club evening
for fourteen- to sixteen-year-olds. Towards the end of the
meeting we broke into groups to pray for one another.
First we shared around the group the needs we had.
In the main the youngsters were worried about school
examinations or relationships with their parents. When
it came to my turn I found it perplexing to know what
to say. I wanted to be honest and yet be relevant to
those I was with. Eventually I told them I was writing
a book about fathering and had hit a difficult patch. One
very astute teenager looked at me and said: 'Maybe that's
because you're a mother and not a father.' Of course he
was right. To be a woman and write about fathering may
seem rather presumptuous.

My reasons are simple. I am convinced that fathers are
much more important than most of us appreciate; that they
are a threatened species; that it behoves us all to do what
we can to save the situation. Also, I feel that sometimes
it is easier to evaluate a problem and find a solution when
one is at a distance rather than when one is too close to
see 'the wood for the trees'.

Anyone who is involved in counselling those with
emotional difficulties will be aware of how often the
client's relationship with his/her father is relevant to their
problems. In most cases the fathers concerned have been
either absent or abusive. I have rarely counselled anyone
with emotional difficulties who has had a good, satisfying
relationship with their father. I am convinced a father
has an important role to play in family life, and yet the

pain of father loss is becoming more common. 'Fathers are curious people, aloof and mysterious, popping in and out of young lives, often having in common a reputation for being distant and preoccupied with their own affairs.'[1] Christopher Hallowell, who wrote those words, admits that his father was the most influential person in his life, even though he appears to have been emotionally absent. The truth is that the absent father is as influential in his children's lives as is a present, available father. But the latter is for better, the former for worse. Many, even Christian fathers, are struggling to play a real part in their families' lives. In a large church one is in a position to relate to many young couples, and this has made me aware of the problems young fathers are having. In most cases they are caught up in a rat-race which demands so much time and energy that little is left over for any vital input into family life.

Although I have highlighted the problem and the reasons underlying it, I have tried, at the same time, to give some answers to the dilemma we face. My aim has not been to criticise and condemn. My desire is to encourage fathers to recognise their vital place in the family and to help them catch a vision of the blessing their greater involvement would be, not only to their children, but also to themselves. I have listed some suggestions to stimulate some creative action. In the end it is up to the men. If they are sufficiently moved and convinced, they will, I believe, start finding ways around the problems they face.

I owe a debt of gratitude to my husband, David. He has been my honest and best critic, and without his help I would never dare to put pen to paper. I was fortunate in choosing a particularly good father for my children, and many times in the book I have used him to illustrate a point. However, he was not perfect, as he would be quick to tell you. But he loved them very much and often sacrificed time and energy to be with

---

[1]Christopher Hallowell, *Father to the Man* (New York: William Morrow, 1987), pp. 14–15.

them. It is for that reason that I gratefully dedicate this book to him.

I would like to thank the Rev. Johan Candelin, who invited me to address a 'men only' meeting in Kokkola, Finland, on the subject of fathering, which started the thinking that led to this book. Also, I am grateful to Jeremy Marks, Director of Courage Trust, who despite a very busy schedule took time to read and comment on the manuscript.

Steven Spielberg's magical film *Hook* is about the now grown-up Peter Pan, who is so caught up in the world of 'big business' that he has lost touch with the boy he once was. Neglect of his family and a string of broken promises causes his wife, Moira, to tell him some home truths – home truths which should be heard by all parents: 'We have a few special years with our children when they are the ones who want us around. After that you are going to be running after them for a bit of attention. So, fast Peter – it's a few years and it's over. You are not being careful and you are missing it.'

Peter came near to losing his children through his short-sightedness. Captain Hook, the epitome of evil, steals them away. The now elderly Wendy Darling tries to awaken Peter to his responsibility. She utters words which are true for fathers everywhere: 'Only you can save your children.'

1

THE IMPORTANCE OF A FATHER

'Lost Boys', a recent television programme in the *Everyman* series, featured three men sharing their grief and pain at the loss of a father. John's father died when he was about ten; David's had left home; and although Roger's father had never left him, he had been emotionally unavailable to his son. Roger observed that the longing of a son for his father is too often never articulated: 'A lot of men are wandering around with a hole inside them still longing for something they didn't have.'[1]

The vital role a father plays in the life of his children too frequently goes unrecognised by society. The story about James Boswell, the biographer of Samuel Johnson, demonstrates the significant part a father may play in the life of his son although the father may never realise it. Boswell often referred to a special day in his childhood when his father took him fishing. He spoke of the different things his father had taught him during that day together. Someone decided to check out Boswell's story in his father's journal, to see how *he* had perceived the outing. Only one entry was found against the date, which ran as follows: 'Gone fishing today with my son; a day wasted.'[2] What a tragic comment! How could any father imagine that a day spent in the company of his son was a day wasted!

However, not every father is as ignorant of the important

[1] *Everyman*, 'Lost Boys', BBC1, 29 November 1992.
[2] Gordon MacDonald, *The Effective Father* (Crowborough: Highland Books, 1989), p. 79.

place he holds in his son's life. Another man who spent a day fishing with his son wrote these words:

> Yes sir, I took my boy a-fishin'. Sure, his mother told me to, but besides, I kind of done it 'cause it seemed the thing to do.
>
> It's a heap more fun a-fishin' when I'm out there with my son, 'cause we really get acquainted through a little fishin' fun.
>
> When my creel of life is empty, and my life's line sort of worn, I shall always keep rememberin' that first early summer morn when I took my boy a-fishin', and I really learned the joy that comes to every father when he really knows his boy.[1]

I heard a father recently describe the interest shown by his young family the moment he makes a move to do something. A chorus of voices want to know where he is going. 'Just going to put the car in the garage,' he may respond. With that four little bodies hurl themselves upon him, shouting: 'Take me with you, Daddy.'

To do something together with Dad is for many children the highlight of the day. Blessed is the family where the father knows this. Sadly, his role is being gradually undermined in many circles today. Father is viewed solely as the provider of funds to keep the family housed, clothed and fed. More tragic still, in some sections of society he is even regarded as unnecessary to the ongoing life of his child – the father's value is limited solely to the sperm he produces for conception.

God's view of fathers

With the exception of a few of the minor prophets, every book in the Bible mentions fathering. It is mentioned many

[1] Herbert V. Prochnow and Herbert V. Prochnow, Jr, *Jokes, Quotes and One-Liners* (Wellingborough: Thorsons Publishing Group, 1987), p. 410.

more times than mothering. God calls himself a Father to his people. He exemplifies a type of parenting which is intimately involved in the ongoing life of his family. The Creator set mankind in families and arranged matters so that every family has both a father and mother.

Preparing for his only Son, Jesus, to be incarnate on the earth, God the Father went to great lengths to ensure that Jesus would have a human father responsible for his protection through the crucial years of childhood. The first coming of Jesus was heralded by heightened supernatural activity: angelic visitations, prophetic utterances, dreams and visions. Mary received one such visitation to prepare her for the birth of Jesus. But Joseph received four important messages to ensure that he carried out his paternal responsibilities to Jesus. In the first dream the Lord commanded him to take Mary as his wife, and so ensured the security of a mother and a father for his son (Matt. 1:20). Secondly, an angel appeared in order to tell Joseph to escape to Egypt (Matt. 2:13), and later another appeared and told him it was now safe to return (Matt. 2:20). Finally, through a dream Joseph was warned that Archelaus was 'reigning in Judea in place of his father Herod', so he went instead to live in Galilee (Matt. 2:22).[1] Through these supernatural revelations God ensured that Jesus would be adequately parented.

Children need a father

Having a father who is concerned for and intimately involved in his child's life is vital for a child's well-being. Without such a father figure a child suffers many different consequences. Some of these will be discussed in a later chapter. A child without a father often grows up without a sense of direction to his life. A father opens the door for the child to the world outside the home. At the right time

[1] Mary Pytches, *Yesterday's Child* (London: Hodder & Stoughton, 1990), pp. 29–30.

he should lead the child through that door to encourage him in the right direction, while remaining on hand if needed. Without such help and guidance a child may find himself rudderless on the vast and stormy ocean of life.

Newspapers are mostly the bearers of bad news, and people become inured to what they read, that is, until we read about crimes which are unthinkable in their brutality and which we never imagined could be perpetrated by young people. Recently, the country has been shocked to the core by the ruthless murder of a two-year-old child. Two ten-year-old boys are currently being charged with his murder.

The headlines of a recent national newspaper ran: YOUNG TEARAWAYS 'A NATIONAL PROBLEM'. Dr Masud Hoghughi, director of the Aycliffe Centre for Children, reported that the behaviour of problem adolescents was deteriorating to the point where they have gone severely wrong: 'There is something really quite frightening about some of the things that are happening in these children's structures.' He went on to say that these youngsters have no attachment to the norms and standards of the rest of society: 'Frankly they don't give a damn. They have nothing to lose and they have even less to gain by conforming . . .'[1]

One wonders whatever has gone wrong in our society that children are so out of control. Are fathers in any way responsible for the dire state of affairs headlined in our daily newspapers? A recent Christian survey found that the average father spent three minutes a day talking to his son or daughter. The same child watched three hours of television a day.[2]

Certainly in the Bible we see that a weak father produces unruly sons. Eli is an example of a father who failed to restrain his sons (1 Sam. 3:13). They were behaving wickedly, but Eli only rebuked them mildly for the shocking things they were involved in. Perhaps old Eli had been preoccupied with the holy work of the priesthood. Perhaps

[1] *Daily Telegraph*, 8 September 1992.
[2] *The Times*, 29 June 1991.

he lacked the time and energy to attend to the needs of his sons and had been an emotionally absent father to them.

It would seem that the absence of effective fathering, whether from weakness, preoccupation, sickness, lack of interest or marriage breakdown, can produce the situation that Dr Hoghughi was describing. Statistically, we know that more children than ever today are growing up with one missing parent. A father may be totally absent through death or divorce. Or, like Roger's father, he may be around but not emotionally available for the child, with the result that no intimate and meaningful relationship is ever formed.

The over-committed father

Many fathers are too busy to do an effective parenting job. Writing about the absent-father syndrome in America, the family therapist Charles Williams says that corporate America has certainly contributed to this phenomenon, and that men have allowed themselves to be forced into unreasonably long working hours. This has gradually increased from the traditional forty-hour week to sixty, seventy and even eighty hours, if needed. 'In a sense,' he comments, 'we have sold out to Corporate America.'[1]

America is not the only greedy country that allows her business companies to demand more than their fair share of a man's time. I recently sat watching Jenny nursing her four-month-old baby girl while her toddler son brandished his sword at an imaginary enemy. It was an attractive family scene except for the absence of Steve. He was away, busy earning the money to pay the bills. 'Well, that's normal,' you say. And of course it is. There would be no real problem had Steve been coming home at six that evening in time to play with his children for a while. But Steve never gets home before eight in the evening, and he leaves early in the morning. He sees his children at

[1] D. Charles Williams, *Forever a Father* (Wheaton, Ill.: Victor Books, 1991), p. 13.

the weekends and for a few weeks' holiday in the year. He feels trapped by the circumstances of his life, but can see no way of changing them. Steve is a Christian, and every time he has a holiday and gets to know his children he tells his wife he is going to make a new effort to get home earlier. But as soon as he gets back to work the strident demands of his job are shouting far louder than the silent demands of his children.

Steve's dilemma is faced by far too many fathers in our society today. Fearing the consequences if they don't, these men give their time and energy, during the best years of life, to business corporations, forfeiting all the joy of being an available, approachable father to their children. Inaccessible for so much of the time, they are unapproachable the rest of their time through sheer exhaustion.

Some fathers are emotionally absent due to ignorance and poor modelling from their own parents. Some are too hurt themselves to give the love and affection needed to satisfy a small child. My own father was a reserved man of few words. My mother would complain that he could sit silently for hours on end, or work in solitude in the greenhouse all day. When he died, aged ninety-two, I felt almost as if I was mourning the loss of a father I never knew. An only child himself, he had never learned the art of good communication. My clearest childhood memories of my father are of him coming home from work exhausted. Soon he was slumped in his chair, reading his newspaper. Only his legs were visible my side of the paper as gradually it flattened on his sleeping form. If ever I refer to this memory in my lecturing, I can guarantee many will approach me later to share the pain of a similar father. We could form a pretty big club!

The absent father

However hard it is for Jenny to cope with two small children and a relatively absent husband, it would be far more difficult for her to cope totally without her husband and the father of her children. Yet many women find themselves in such a position. Some 1987 statistics suggest that with current divorce trends it is likely that one in three recent marriages will end in divorce and that one in five children under sixteen will experience their parents' divorce – a total of over 150,000 children each year in England and Wales.[1] Usually it is the mother who is granted care of the children and it is the husband who leaves home. Although they probably mean to keep in touch with their children too many separated fathers lose contact after the first few years. Others, of course, find the hassle from the mother too difficult to overcome.

There are other reasons for the absent-father syndrome which we will examine in more depth later. Whatever the cause, and whatever the degree of absence, however, the effect upon the children is as negative as a good father's presence is positive.

In the counselling room

I have become increasingly aware of the dimension of this problem in the counselling room. Probably ninety per cent of all the people I have counselled over the past ten years have been affected in some negative way by the kind of relationship they had with their fathers.

When Eric first came for help, he reminded me of a wounded dog. His wife told me that she sometimes felt as if she was married to a hurt child. He was outwardly a successful man, with a good mind, an interesting job and a lovely family. But inwardly he felt a failure. He had a low self-image which affected everything he did. He lacked initiative, could not make friends, suffered from feelings of frustration, and continually compared himself unfavourably with others. His story, though sad, was not unusual. The predominant memories of his childhood

---

[1] Lisa Parkinson, 'Parents, children and divorce', in Richard Whitfield (ed.), *Families Matter* (Basingstoke: Marshall Pickering, 1987), p. 151.

were unhappy ones. His father had been mostly absent, but whenever present he was critical, and abusive to his children. His mother, subdued and weakened by her bullying husband, had little energy left to comfort her son. This shy, diffident boy had needed, as does every child, the strong masculine touch from his father to support, encourage and affirm him. But that basic human right was denied him, and now he sat in our counselling office confessing in undertones that sometimes he felt like killing himself. 'If only Dad had been different!'

'If only . . .' are words frequently heard when counselling people who have been robbed of something they instinctively feel they had a right to. 'If only my Dad would give me a hug,' said Dick when asked what he wanted from his parents. He had turned up on his youth leader's doorstep one evening, saying he was miserable. After a cup of coffee and a bit of a chat he opened up to his friend and confessed to needing his Dad: 'I just want him to notice me. If only he would give me a hug now and again.' Encouragement, affection and affirmation are what a teenager needs from his father, but those demands require time, and that is the one commodity most fathers do not possess, though many would wish they did.

One family asked for counselling because the eldest daughter was constantly at loggerheads with her mother. Though there were underlying causes for this difficulty, the main trigger was the father's recent and unusual absence from home for reasons of business. On one occasion we had asked the eldest child to speak about her feelings. She talked about not being understood by her mother and of her sibling being favoured over her, and then she sighed and said: 'If only Dad were at home more.' At this Dad looked stricken: 'You know I want to be at home, but there is nothing I can do right now.' The young girl had always relied upon her Dad to be totally just and fair in a potentially difficult situation. His absence had taken away that controlling influence and the pot had boiled over. But he was trapped and caught up in the demanding world of business.

Experience as a parent

This sense of longing for a relationship with one's father, and the resulting emptiness when it doesn't happen, has persuaded me that fathers are more important to their children than our society would lead us to believe. The concern God showed when he revealed his will to Joseph, as the earthly father of Jesus, is another strong argument. If I needed more persuasion, the experience of watching my own daughters relating to their father over the past thirty years would be enough.

When they were small, the greatest treat was Saturday morning story-time, tucked up in bed next to Dad. The greatest comfort was to curl up on his lap when they felt poorly. In their teens the greatest adventure was to persuade him to take them shopping! Now, as adults, 'Will Dad be home?' is the question asked when they are coming with their families for a visit. Their pride and joy in their father's company is obvious, and is being passed on down to their children. Recently we took our four-year-old grandson out to lunch with his parents and a visiting friend of ours. Zachery was sitting in the back of our car while the visitor got into the front. David and I greeted our friend. There was a brief pause, and then a loud voice from the back announced proudly, 'And I'm Zachery, my grandfather's grandson.'

Father – a key person

While reflecting on his father, the Harvard psychologist Samuel Osherson realised that he had found the man he had been searching for, the father who, more by his absence than his presence, was the key to the sense of emptiness and vulnerability in his life.[1] Dad may be a key factor in one's emotional difficulties. He is also a key to his child's happiness and security. Many fathers are ignorant of their vital role:

[1] Samuel Osherson, *Finding Our Fathers* (New York: Ballantine Books, 1986), p. x.

Sons are a heritage from the Lord, children a reward from him. Like arrows in the hands of a warrior are sons born in one's youth. Blessed is the man whose quiver is full of them. They will not be put to shame when they contend with their enemies in the gate.

(Ps. 127:3–5)

Sons and daughters were intended by God to be a father's pride and joy. They were considered to be a blessing; a reward from God. Yet many men still contend that they are doing the best thing for their children by working eighty hours a week absent from home. Charles Williams sees a trend, at least in the United States, away from this destructive scenario:

Men seem to want to be home more instead of working sixty or seventy hours each week. Fathers are less willing to remain in jobs where they are travelling five days per week. They are even accepting lesser paying jobs and postponing career promotions to spend more time at home with their children. Some are realizing the necessity of lowering their standard of living in order to spend this valuable time with their families.[1]

May this trend spread to the United Kingdom also, because, whether we realise it or not, our children need their fathers.

Some men are intuitively aware of their importance and take steps to incorporate their children into their busy schedule. The successful American comedian Bill Cosby admits that he makes a lot of money and gives a lot of it to charities, 'But', he says, 'I've given all of myself to my wife and kids, and that's the best donation I'll ever make.'[2]

Another wise father gave a gift to his son in the form of a promise note. It read: 'To my dear son: In the New Year, I shall give you one hour of each weekday, and two hours of my Sundays, to be yours and to be used as you

[1] Williams, *Forever a Father*, p. 29.
[2] Bill Cosby, *Fatherhood* (Reading: Bantam Books, 1986), p. 85.

want them, without interference of any kind whatsoever.
– Your Father.'[1] That note had more real value to the son
than any promise of money.

The award-winning film *Kramer vs. Kramer* was primarily about a couple's battle against one another for the
custody of their son. However, to my mind the stronger
theme was the amazing conversion of Ted, played by
Dustin Hoffman, from being merely a man who had
fathered a child to being a fully participating parent of
a little boy. At the end of her tether and suicidal, Joanna,
the mother, walks out on her son Billy, leaving him to be
looked after by Ted. This husband is an ambitious young
man, consumed by his job, who expected his family to
survive his preoccupation with 'getting to the top'. When
his wife deserted him he was left with a small child needing
his attention, and a job that demanded twenty-five hours
out of every twenty-four. For eight months he battled
with his son's demand for a father and his boss's demand
for a dedicated workaholic. Thankfully, his love for his
son won over his desire to reach the top. His son's need
caused him to make the choice that freed him to become
a real father.

Many fathers never recognise the need of a son or
daughter for their presence. They believe that their duty
has been fully executed when they pay the bills. They may
be distracted from seeing the truth by preoccupation and
exhaustion. They may even be backed up by wives who
have grown accustomed to absentee husbands, or who are
silenced by the fear of losing him if 'unreasonable family
demands' are made upon him. But whether they recognise
it or not, every child needs his father as much as little Billy
Kramer needed his.

[1] Prochnow and Prochnow, *Jokes, Quotes and One-Liners*, p.
381.

2

SOCIAL REASONS FOR
THE ABSENT FATHER

> Our struggle is not against flesh and blood, but against
> the rulers, against the authorities, against the powers of
> this dark world and against the spiritual forces of evil in
> the heavenly realms. (Eph. 6:12)

Every Christian is aware that he or she is involved in a
battle. At times it seems to be personified in a human
being, at other times social structures. Behind whichever it
may be, there is an evil influence which seeks to undermine
all that is wholesome and godly. The battle is often so sub-
tle that we have been unaware that we have been gradually
losing ground to the enemy. The Bible tells us that 'the
whole world is under the control of the evil one' (1 John
5:19). A moment's reflection convinces us of that truth.

Divorce, for example, is on the increase and can occur
for no better reason than boredom. 'The rate of increase
of Divorce over the last twenty years has been 400% . . .
By the year 2000 1 in 5 of the population will have been
married twice.'[1] Slowly the security of family life is being
eroded, and Christians are among those being sucked into
the trend.

Child abuse is another example. When yet another case
is uncovered, it shocks us; but we never hear about the
majority of cases, because the child is either too scared

[1] Richard Whitfield, 'Child protection, marriage and the family',
in Richard Whitfield (ed.), *Families Matter* (Basingstoke: Marshall Pickering, 1987), p. 4.

to tell or it is done in such a way as to make the child think it is normal.

A woman came up to me after a seminar on child abuse. She told me that she had come because her son was a homosexual. She had wondered if he could have been abused as a child. 'But after hearing you speak,' she said, 'I think perhaps I was abused.' She then described what she had endured at the hands of her father. Although he had not in fact raped her, he had, throughout her childhood, molested her in a way which would have been considered sexual abuse by any social worker.

We try to comfort ourselves, hoping that Christians are not involved in such things. But in fact it would seem that even they are not free of such perversions. In a recent US survey it was found that ninety per cent of the reported child-abuse victims were female, and that fathers or stepfathers were the most common offenders. Pastors had reported forty-eight per cent of the cases and counsellors fifty-six per cent.[1] This suggests that Christian families are almost as much affected as non-Christian. It is hard to bury our heads in the sand after such information.

A young woman suffering from sexual problems recently told me that her father, a pastor, used to touch her very inappropriately when she was nearing puberty. On another occasion, while speaking about family life at a ladies' meeting, a young girl had to be taken out. I had mentioned the problem of incest in some homes, and she had begun to sob. Apparently her father, a Christian doctor, had violated her sexually throughout her childhood.

Home life is under threat! It is estimated that half our married couples with small children are both out working. Forty per cent of today's work-force are women, compared with thirty per cent in the 1950s. The proportion of married women who go out to work has increased sevenfold since the early 1920s.[2] The physically and emotionally present

---

[1] Paula Sandford, *Healing Victims of Sexual Abuse* (Oklahoma: Victory House, 1988), p. ix.
[2] *Families Matter*, p. 5.

mother is fast disappearing from our homes. Working mothers are forced to leave their children with other care-givers, and when they do come home they are often too tired to be as patient and loving as they would like to be.

An Abortion Law was passed in 1967 which in fact enabled women to get an abortion almost on demand, even though parliament assured us that this would not happen. A war is being waged on the unborn child which society does not want to know about:

> In the semantic revolution the unborn child becomes 'the contents of the womb', or 'a blob of jelly', abortion 'termination of a pregnancy', paedophilia 'young love', the illegitimate child 'a love child' and the homosexual 'gay'. Thus the unthinkable becomes palatable; everything is relative and nothing normative.[1]

That quotation demonstrates the way we try to shield ourselves from so many uncomfortable truths by a clever use of words.

Satan is waging a war against the nuclear family, whose well-being is foundational to the health of any nation. God purposed for children to be nurtured and prepared for adult life in a home and within a family. However, in the present climate this task is becoming more and more difficult. Our men face a particularly intense struggle to be good fathers to their children. Many fathers are losing ground and losing heart. But some are not even aware that there is a battle; they are just caught up in the rat-race, accepting that this is the way it has to be and hoping the children will survive. Others, like Jenny's husband Steve, are aware of the dangers but feel helpless to prevent themselves from gradually slipping out of their children's lives as the ever-increasing work-load becomes more and more demanding.

It is helpful at times to look at the root causes behind certain trends. Understanding alone will not change a

[1] ibid., p. 24.

situation, but insight often releases energy to make some appropriate changes. It is also true that opening up a problem to the light releases a measure of healing. Satan prefers to keep us in darkness and ignorance, because in that way he can keep us captives to the circumstances.

Though we could never hope to identify every cause for the absent-father syndrome, some are relatively obvious ones and worth mentioning.

Historical causes

This is always a safe place to begin. History can be interesting but happily impersonal. Nevertheless, it can be very enlightening. It is often possible to gain a new slant on a problem when it is seen in the light of past events.

Two world wars

This century has been marked by two world wars. Inevitably, war changes people's lives. With so many men away, it was left to the women to work in the factories. During the First World War, women found themselves thrust into a man's world and surprised themselves by their capabilities outside the home. Consequently, in many countries in Europe women were given the vote for the first time. While women came to the rescue at home, the men were being decimated at the front. During the First World War in particular, the casualties were enormous: 'A whole generation of men was lost, and future generations were blighted as a result. Nine million people were killed and seventeen million were wounded, of whom a third became invalids. Four million women were widowed, twice as many children were orphaned.'[1]

Two significant results of this war were that women had to step into men's shoes, and millions of children were condemned to grow up fatherless.

[1] *Chronicle of the World* (London: Longman/Chronicle Communications), p. 1072.

The Great Depression
Then in 1932 came the Great Depression, rendering two million Britons out of work. In America the total rose to fourteen million. For men who had considered their most important role to be a provider for the family, this was both disheartening and depressing; it robbed men of confidence in their paternal abilities and responsibilities.

At the countdown to the Second World War there were five million unemployed in Germany who were pinning their hopes on Adolf Hitler. Once again, in Britain the women valiantly came to the fore, showing their strength and stamina in factories, on the land, and in the forces. They coped bravely, unsupported by the men, making do on the 'rations', sleeping in air-raid shelters, and giving their all to the war effort. Meanwhile the men were being ravaged at the front. There were over fifty million casualties. Once again thousands of children were to grow up never knowing a father's presence.

Two world wars and a major depression crushed the men of Europe and America. Women were thrust to the fore, and many children were robbed of their right to grow up with two parents to care for them. What is more, two generations of boys grew up without any model of good fathering to prepare them for parenthood.

Social and cultural causes

Contraception
In the 1950s cheap and reliable forms of contraception were developed which made it possible for couples to delay having children. This allowed women to enter careers previously reserved for men. Contraception also meant that marriage ceased to be the reason for a couple to set up a household together. They could live together for as long as it suited them without the risk of having children, which would have forced them into a marriage relationship. Men and women began to feel they had a right to happiness and to self-fulfilment. Thus the changing

status of women and the personal aspirations of society began to challenge family life. 'Future historians may well decide that it was human relationships that were the most profoundly changed by all the developments of the post-war years.'[1]

The women's movement

As we have seen, the woman's role has changed dramatically in the last hundred years. In the previous century the woman's place was largely in the home. Tennyson could write in his 'Princess Ida':

> Man for the field and woman for the hearth,
> Man for the sword and for the needle she;
> Man with the head and woman with the heart
> Man to command and woman to obey
> All else confusion.[2]

The 1870 Education Act provided an elementary education for girls and boys equally. London University was the first to admit women, in 1848; but in 1872 Girton College was established in Cambridge, and in 1879 Oxford followed suit with Somerville and Lady Margaret Hall. However, even though many women were excelling in achieving real academic success, they were debarred from taking degrees until after the First World War. In 1919 the Sex Disqualification (Removal) Act made it illegal to continue the debarring of woman from employment on grounds of their sex.

The First World War had played an important part in the emancipation of women, though full equality did not actually come until 1928 when all British women over the age of twenty-one were given the vote. Politically, at least, women were now considered to be equal with men. It would seem, however, that although women had apparently been given the same educational and

---

[1] *Chronicle of the World*, p. 1137.
[2] M. C. James, *GCE O-level Passbook: History* (Maidenhead: Intercontinental Book Productions, 1976), p. 141.

professional opportunities as men, the parity women desired was still in effect not forthcoming.

Feminism

By 1970 a militant feminist movement had grown out of the women's movement. The well-known feminist Germaine Greer wrote: 'The new emphasis is different. The genteel middle-class ladies clamoured for reform, now ungenteel middle-class women are calling for revolution.'[1] It is true that changes were still needed. For many women life was not fair. Men, suffering from a 'complex' of male superiority, still blocked promotion of women in the work-place. Women still suffered from sexual harassment and cruelty, and many felt humiliated by being treated as sex symbols. Though these things needed to be tackled, nevertheless this revolutionary approach to the problem was to pose a real threat to the life of the nuclear family. It was different from the women's movement which had previously struggled to change the unfair status of women in society. Although the cry for equal opportunities was similar, and appeared reasonable in the light of continuing sexual discrimination, there was an increasing disregard for the welfare of children and the maintenance of family life. Germaine Greer admits that family life is being sacrificed to the demand for equality. In fact, Patricia Morgan draws the conclusion that

> the one 'popular' solution advocated for all women has been uninterrupted full-time work with full-time creches. Equality of outcome is the end to which all other possible female choices and all consideration of anybody else, including children, are subordinated. Insofar as 'family policy' is perceived chiefly as a 'women's issue', its only reference to parental roles is in terms of how women can resist and fight the demands of home and children.[2]

[1] Germaine Greer, *The Female Eunuch* (London: Grafton Books, 1970), p. 11.
[2] Patricia Morgan, in Whitfield (ed.), *Families Matter*, p. 32.

The opponents of earlier women's movements had seen into the future and warned that women's emancipation would result in the end of marriage, and of morality. Greer confirms this fear: 'their extremism was more clear-sighted than the woolly benevolence of liberals and humanists, who thought that giving women a measure of freedom would not upset anything. When we reap the harvest which the unwitting suffragettes sowed we shall see that the anti-feminists were after all right.'[1]

Thus marriage and family life have been viewed by the extreme feminists as an impediment to the pursuit of freedom, independence and the equality of women. They have made no pretence about their attitude: 'If women are to effect a significant amelioration in their condition it seems obvious that they must refuse to marry.'[2] Their attitude to the opposite sex has ranged from chronic dislike to vitriolic hatred. Although a man is still needed for his sperm, the feminist would deny him the right to be the father his child needs, fearing that his participation would become a means to exert control and dominance. The feminist

> asserts that just as the means of production must be returned to the rightful producers (the proletariat), so the female body and its products must be returned exclusively to the woman. Not only must no man know his own child, but none shall have any claims or interest in children or foetuses that are not held (or terminated) at the will of the mother.

The author of those words, commenting that there is no sadness over the rising divorce rate or the illegitimacy figures, goes on: 'The "disappearing parent", usually the father, should be sped on his way as an encouraging prelude to a general disestablishment of male ties to families.'[3] After years of deliberation, the law courts

[1] Greer, *The Female Eunuch*, p. 22.
[2] ibid., p. 319.
[3] Patricia Morgan, in Whitfield (ed.), *Families Matter*, p. 34.

upheld the feminist demands to undermine the rights of the father regarding the unborn child. In 1981 the European Court of Justice confirmed that the father has no right to be consulted respecting the termination of pregnancy.

A recent headline in a national newspaper read: 'WHO NEEDS A FATHER ANYWAY?' The article was about Baby J., who is a child of our times. His mother chose his father from a sperm bank; now 'he is being reared on State benefits'. Jessica Davies, commenting on the article, says that the state is the only father such children will know – and what sort of father is that? Davies admits to being old-fashioned: 'I imagine a society peopled by children like Baby J – boys and girls who have never known what it means to have a real father – and I am filled with dismay.'[1]

The feminist movement has many sympathetic supporters who are responding to their struggle against unfairness. For the most part these genuine supporters are unaware of the threat the revolutionary feminist poses to marriage, family life and the position of a father in relation to his child. Children without a father's involvement, as we shall see in a later chapter, may show a variety of disturbances, some of which are very costly to our society as a whole. Truancy, delinquency and lack of respect for the older generation are common occurrences, and point to a breakdown in family relationships.

The media

In the study of delinquency and crime, the sociologist Norman Dennis and the psychologist George Erdos point to the collapse of family life, not poverty or unemployment, as the main cause of the problem. They draw attention to the part the media have played in the breakdown of the family, which is the cornerstone of any free society. According to Dennis and Erdos, the media have too often promoted views held by minority sections of the

[1] *Daily Mail*, Friday 19 February 1993.

population who have elevated themselves above common sense and the findings of statistical surveys.

In 1960 things began changing radically. A thorough remoulding of attitudes was effected. By the 1990s many students, the opinion-formers of the future, held the view that 'To be pre-committed "for a life-time" and "for better or worse" to render unpaid services to another was an eccentric notion that had never worked in practice, and all they were doing was discarding an oppressive ideology.'[1]

Erdos and Dennis cite Radio 4 as having been the citadel of British conventional values for thirty years or more. Within that citadel *Woman's Hour* was a stronghold of respectability and an upholder of family morality. Yet a more recent presenter of *Woman's Hour* publicly stated her conviction that marriage was an 'insult' – 'Women shouldn't touch it.' In her opinion marriage had made her a 'legal prostitute'.[2]

Opinion-formers who were mainly based in places of higher education made their influence felt most widely through serious newspapers and discussion programmes: '[Their] prime commitment was to draw attention to, and remedy, the evils associated with the system of life-long monogamy.' These ideas were broadcast even though factual surveys showed 'that on average the life-long socially-certified monogamous family on the pre-1960 pattern was better for children than any one of a variety of alternatives'.[3]

It is indisputable that in recent years the cinema, television, radio and newspapers have not been a means of promoting family life or of presenting a healthy masculine image. It is rare to see an adult video which does not feature fornication, adultery or divorce as if they were the norm. A film depicting ordinary family life would be deemed uninteresting and with no box-office draw.

[1] Norman Dennis and George Erdos, *Families Without Fatherhood* (London: IEA Health and Welfare Unit, 1992), p. 35.
[2] ibid., p. 35 (quoting J. Murray, *Options*, 1992, p. 8).
[3] ibid., p. 33.

The media advertise tantalising alternatives to long-term family commitment – alternatives which are hard to resist. Before 1960, sexual alliances outside of marriage were usually concealed. When uncovered they were viewed as shameful. Yet when the former Vice-President of the USA, Dan Quayle, recently attacked a television series called *Murphy Brown* because Murphy, representing a liberal, independent woman, decided to have a baby without getting married, he was mocked as a 'fuddy duddy' who stood for 'old-fashioned values'. Dan Quayle felt that it should not have been presented as just 'another lifestyle choice', nor should it have been shown at prime viewing time; but such conservative views were definitely in the minority as far as the media were concerned. Now and again there are some exceptions, of which the popular *Cosby Show* is one. It portrays family life in a healthy, normal light. Also some of the 'watch-dog' programmes are pro-family and attempt to protect the interests of society.

We cannot pretend that the media, and in particular television, do not have tremendous influence upon people's attitudes, and more importantly upon the formation of children's minds. The three hours of TV which the average child watches daily must have an impact upon him. The macho man is the masculine image most popularly portrayed on the screen. The heroes of our children are the Clint Eastwoods and the Arnold Schwarzeneggers; unfeeling, powerful men. The weak and stupid are those our children are taught to despise. Rarely do we see a good, healthy, normal male image portrayed through the media; a man who has a good sense of humour, who copes with the ups and downs of living, who is loving and sensitive, who can be strong but is not afraid of weakness.

Fashionable trends

Our society reeks with unhealthy attitudes that trap many men. These attitudes lead them to defeat in their personal lives, marriages and opportunities as fathers. The conscientious father needs to take a hard look at what he is being taught by society and determine not to let the 'system' squeeze him into its mould.[1]

The attitudes which especially need examining are those which denigrate the family as being of secondary importance to a man's work or hobbies; those which laugh at faithfulness and decry it as being boring and not in a man's best interests; those which place personal happiness and fulfilment above the security and well-being of one's family; those which view religion as unnecessary or at best a female whim.

Individualism

One prevalent twentieth-century attitude which has been promoted by some secular psychologies is that of radical individualism. 'Psychologists like Alfred Maslow have helped to popularise this notion, so that the search for individual fulfilment is now perhaps the dominant feature of western culture.' This attitude has a negative effect upon healthy family life

in which members are committed to each other, but where the commitment is not so intense that the other person feels stifled. Members care for one another but also allow each other to breathe. There is a balance between relationships and personal autonomy. The self-please ethic wrecks that balance. Instead of commitment it encourages rejection, instead of respect for the other's autonomy it encourages emotional clinging. It does that in marriage and in parenting.[2]

Radical individualism leads people to live for themselves alone. The joy of sacrificially giving oneself to another and learning to love one's neighbour as oneself is lost. Such

---

[1] Josh McDowell and Dr Norm Wakefield, *The Dad Difference* (San Bernardino: Here's Life Publishers, 1989), p. 50.
[2] Michael Moynagh, *Home to Home* (London: Daybreak, 1990), p. 28.

people rate 'aloneness' higher than living in relatedness to others. By so doing they miss not only the comfort and support of a close relationship, but also the challenges and changes which such a relationship can bring to one.

A recent survey shows that solo living is becoming very fashionable today. Millions of people are opting for its freedom. The survey shows that one in four households in Britain is now a single-person unit; that is more than six million people.[1] This tendency is bound to give rise to more people opting for sex outside marriage, without its restraints and responsibilities. Divorce becomes increasingly attractive since marriage has been wrongly viewed as a means of self-gratification.

The work ethic
Work was God's idea. He put man in the Garden of Eden to work it and take care of it. Work provides both men and women with a sense of significance, and in many instances real satisfaction. For single or childless women, employment is often a necessary part of their lives. Nor should the idea of work be linked only to employment. Married women who have chosen to stay at home and care for a family are also working and making a valuable contribution to society. In addition, such women often serve the community in a voluntary capacity during the hours their children are at school.

For the married man, work brings in the income by which he houses, feeds, clothes and educates his family. Without it he begins to lose his sense of purpose. Yet, unavoidably, when a man is employed his work-place is where he spends the major part of his life. He often talks more with those he works with than with his own wife and children. Most of his mental, emotional and physical energy is expended at work. Sometimes, as already mentioned, the job demands more than a forty-hour week and at this point work becomes the enemy instead of the ally of family life. Companies make a constant demand

[1] *Daily Telegraph*, 15 September 1992.

for results, and in the throes of enormous competition expect that an employee will give his last ounce of blood for their gain. Few big businesses take into consideration a man's need to spend quality time with his family. If he wants to get on, he must sacrifice the family; he cannot have both.

Recently, I flew back on a Sunday from a conference in Europe. It was a shock to find I was travelling with a plane-load of men. I sat next to a man who spent the entire journey writing up the minutes of the meeting he had been attending in Finland. I listened in to the conversation between two men in the seats behind me. They were talking animatedly about plans to begin a new engineering enterprise. I had only a few days previously been speaking to nearly three hundred men on the subject of fathering. Now I found myself seated on a plane with men who should have been at home with their families instead of giving up their precious weekends to the demands of business.

Even when they are at home, companies still think they have a right to an employee's time. I heard recently of a young man who was out one evening attending a church meeting. While he was out his boss rang. When his wife explained that her husband was out at a church meeting the boss responded: 'What for? He should be at home doing his paperwork.' The person who told this story expressed the opinion that most big business corporations have an idolatrous drive for power and success, and other interests such as home, family, hobbies and friendships must be sacrificed on their greedy altar.

The global village

Since the end of the last war, the concept of the 'global village' has come into being. Communications have improved to such an extent that we can be made aware of what is going on in the furthest corner of the world within seconds. Newer and faster methods of transport mean that a man can be the other side of the world within hours, with the result that the pace and scope of the work-place has changed. Dad could be having his breakfast with his children in Birmingham and be flying into Berlin by lunch-time.

The tension between the demands of work and the needs of the family is one faced by most men in our society today, and needs to be examined. There are certainly no easy answers, but later in the book I will list some suggestions which may give clues as to a way through the impasse.

These social and cultural pressures often leave a man wounded and exhausted. Jesus knew that it would be like this, and for this reason he prayed for his disciples just before he died: 'My prayer is not that you take them out of the world but that you protect them from the evil one. They are not of the world, even as I am not of it' (John 17:15–16). Jesus knew that the values of the world in which we live would conflict with the values of his kingdom. For this reason he prays for us still: 'Therefore he is able to save completely those who come to God through him, because he always lives to intercede for them' (Heb. 7:25).

Two world wars, economic depression, militant feminism, easy access to contraception, the media, fashionable trends and demanding work schedules may be among some of the social reasons why fathering is under threat today. However, there are other causes of a more personal nature, which may pose an even greater threat.

3

PERSONAL REASONS FOR
THE ABSENT FATHER

The cultural and economic forces which put pressure on
a man and cause him to be an absentee father come from
outside himself. When a cultural or economic pressure
finds a corresponding response within a man's heart, then
it begins to exert an even stronger influence upon him.

The need for significance

The outside pressure of work finds a loud echo within a
man who as a child perceived that he was only loved and
appreciated when he succeeded. This experience will have
built up an inner pressure to achieve. The tendency for
this kind of person is for him to define himself by what
he does. The job can become a way of gaining a feeling
of significance and value. Helping us to understand the
family, Michael Moynagh illustrates the pull work has
upon a man by describing the experience of James, a
consultant at a teaching hospital. From his job he draws
a good income and is highly regarded by many people.
His life has purpose and he is able to help hundreds of
patients. His research has yielded results, and from it
he receives wide acclaim and a sense of achievement.
The compensations for being a husband and father are
small in comparison. He receives no income from it, no
prestige, and his successes are only appreciated by a few.[1]

[1] Michael Moynagh, *Home to Home* (London: Daybreak, 1990),
p. 9.

It is certainly true that if a man is looking for immediate recognition and appreciation for what he does, the home is not the best place to find it. In the chaos of family life there is little time for the handing out of compliments. It is usually much later, when families reflect on their past, that a good father's input to family life is recognised and appreciated. Sometimes it is not truly evaluated while he is this side of the grave.

Man's natural inclination to be self-centred

The prevalent attitude of radical individualism encourages men's (and women's) inherent self-centredness. Human beings are not naturally self-sacrificing and generous. Their fallen nature inclines them to be egocentric and mean. So when the media and the psychologists tell a man that he must do whatever makes him feel fulfilled and actualised as a person, something within him will respond positively. Soon he is planning more time and space for himself. He is irritated by the family's demands upon him and looks upon the time after the day's work is over as exclusively his own. His Saturdays are planned around what he would like to do, and soon he has ceased to think of himself as a person in relation to others for whom God has given him the responsibility for loving, supporting, protecting and equipping. Responsible, self-sacrificing fathers may never be given a medal or a rise, yet not only in heaven will his true greatness be recorded, but his future generations will all rise up to call him blessed.

Fear of intimacy

The majority of men I know tell me that they were never really close to their fathers. 'My Dad couldn't show his feelings' or 'My Dad was away so much' or 'My Dad thought boys should be independent and tough.' These are the sort of reasons given. Consequently, men who experienced little intimacy with their fathers find it difficult to form intimate relationships with their wives and children.

I recently had occasion to pray for a young man who had a stiff and painful neck condition. I laid my hand gently on the back of his neck and began to pray for God's healing. I had only been praying a short while when he suddenly opened his eyes and said to me: 'I don't like people getting close to me.' I quickly moved a pace backwards, thinking that he was referring to me. But then he proceeded to explain himself. He told me that he was under considerable strain with his present girlfriend. He liked her very much and wanted the relationship to become serious, but she was pressing in too close for comfort and it made him want to back off. He said that he had always had a problem with people who had tried to get close to him. I asked him to tell me about his family and his relationship with his parents. He told me that his father had been away a good part of his childhood and that his mother had been rather an unreliable sort of person. In those few short sentences he revealed the most likely reason for his fear of intimacy. He could not allow himself to get too close to people for fear that they would let him down – the pain would be unbearable.

A baby's greatest need in the early months of life is to be able to depend upon the availability of a caring mother figure without too many disturbing interruptions. For every man or woman, this primal experience will have set the scene for all future encounters with intimacy. Following closely on the heels of this experience with mother will be the baby's experience with its father. If he is unavailable for one reason or another, and little or no attachment is made, this will add to the baby's defences against closeness. When a boy fails to connect and identify with the masculinity of his father, and to experience his paternal care, he is left bereft. From henceforth he walks the earth only partially in touch with himself and hardly able to relate to others at any depth, even his own children.

The modern trend which exalts the individual and

popularises solo living compounds the fear of intimacy, whereas we need encouragement to push through the fear barrier. Togetherness and closeness are the factors which give a family true cohesion and strength. Dr Norm Wakefield, lecturer, counsellor and father of five, writes: 'Intimacy – the capacity to be real, open and honest – is a vital part of the communication network that allows biblical insights, emotional resources, sound values and psychological strength to pass from father to child.' He goes on to say that this intimacy originates with God the Father: 'We read in John 1:18 that "No one has ever seen God, but God the only Son, who is at the Father's side, has made him known." In the original wording, the verse speaks of Jesus being in the "bosom" of the Father.'[1] This Hebrew term expresses the deepest possible intimacy.

Lack of courage

Good fathering takes courage and stamina. Many men think nothing of committing themselves to sport or a business enterprise, and often show amazing fortitude and endurance in the face of great difficulties. However, the same men can be cowards when it comes to sacrificial love. When they are faced with the possibility of loving another human being more than they love themselves, they retreat behind the newspaper, the golf club, the pub, the television or the work-place and draw back from the challenge. It takes courage to love. I once heard a man speak on the subject of courage, and he commented on the amount of courage it takes to be a parent. He mentioned the time he first set eyes on his baby daughter. In that moment he realised that for the rest of his life whatever happened to her would affect him deeply. It takes courage to let the heart be so vulnerable to another human being.

'Is there a price to pay for being a good father?' asks

[1] Josh McDowell and Dr Norm Wakefield, *The Dad Difference* (San Bernardino: Here's Life Publishers, 1989), p. 55.

Gordon MacDonald. 'Unquestionably,' is his answer. But he comments that few wish to pay the price which the mandate of effective fatherhood demands. It's just too high for the tastes and disciplines of most men.[1] The price tag is self-sacrifice. The sacrifice of energy, time, sleep, freedom, tidiness and money. Children are life-changing; if this were not so, I would doubt the effectiveness of the parenting. To be a good parent one has to swim courageously against the tide that is pulling one into the whirlpool of self – self-fulfilment, self-actualisation and self-satisfaction.

Good fathering demands time and energy which a man could otherwise have spent on himself. Writing on fatherhood, a young father-to-be, Jocelyn Targett, asks himself a pertinent question which he then seeks to answer truthfully:

> Will I be sad if my baby costs me some of my aspira-
> tions? I think I will, and I think baby is bound to. Having
> a child I'm sure presents the ambitious parent with a
> few inequitable would-you-rathers: would I rather work
> late or feed the tot, leads ultimately to, would I rather
> achieve greatness or be loved overwhelmingly by my
> child for ever more, and I'd choose the love of my
> baby every time . . . but not without in some sense
> disappearing as a human being in my own right. He
> who is not busy, busy being born is busy dying. I am
> not dying but a young and selfish part of me is, and I
> will mourn it when it goes.[2]

Lack of a good role model

Many men find fatherhood difficult because they have never been adequately fathered themselves. We all respond to models and tend to follow the ones we have been given.

[1] Gordon MacDonald, *The Effective Father* (Crowborough: High-land Books, 1989), p. 49.
[2] Jocelyn Targett, in Sean French (ed.), *Fatherhood* (London: Virago, 1992), p. 112.

Samuel and Eli are biblical examples of this. Eli was a priest before the Lord, but his two sons, Hophni and Phinehas, had no regard for the Lord and sinned by treating the Lord's offering with contempt. As already mentioned, Eli knew this was happening but failed to restrain them (1 Sam. 2:12–36). During this time Samuel was growing up and aware of all that was going on in Eli's family. One would have thought that this experience would have made him extra careful to discipline his own sons, but sadly we read later that Samuel's sons did not walk in the ways of their father and turned out very like Hophni and Phinehas (1 Sam. 8:3).

If the only experience a man has had of fathering is of an emotionally distant man who never communicated with him in a meaningful way, then he will most likely relate to his own children in a similar fashion. A man whose father was a workaholic will tend to become a workaholic himself. In response to his wife's complaint that his family never see him, he will probably tell her that he has no alternative, and in any case he turned out all right, and so will they.

Repetition or rebellion are the two responses made by sons of incompetent fathers. Although the rebellious are making an effort to be different, it often does not bear good fruit because it stems from rebellion, which the Bible says is as the sin of witchcraft (1 Sam. 15:23). Both those who rebel and those who repeat the pattern are controlled by the sins of their fathers and need first a revelation and then the power of repentance to break the pattern. Recently a young man told me how his father had received such a revelation. This man had thought that his only value was in providing materially for the family. This he faithfully did, as had his own father before him. It wasn't until his work took him away from home all the week that he realised his real value. His wife told him that apparently his son, then only seven, would start waiting for him to come home on Thursday and keep up his patient vigil until he arrived on Friday evening. It was then that he realised that the pattern he was perpetuating was inadequate and that fathering entailed far more than just material provision. This realisation, and the real sorrow he felt, enabled him to make important changes in the way he related to his family.

However, if a man's father was totally absent through death or divorce, and no other masculine model was present, a man is left not to repeat or rebel but to flounder. Not only does he lack an internal image of a good father, but he may also remain too identified with the feminine. When this happens he becomes a 'soft male', lacking the strength and courage necessary to father well. He may be left with a 'father hunger' which shows itself in homosexual fantasies or dreams – even activities. He may marry but be unable to make a proper separation from his mother, although his wife may be demanding it.

Other young boys who lack a father to separate them from their mother may respond by struggling to separate themselves and do so through rejection of the feminine. They may become 'tough males' who are afraid of showing any of the gentle, more intuitive traits which they associate with the feminine. They are then handicapped in their ability to relate as a true father should.

This lack of a suitable model hinders many of our fathers from doing a good job with their children. Unconsciously, Christians may copy the general trend of society or the male image depicted in the media, not realising that these will always represent 'the world' which Jesus warned us we are not to be a part of. Unfortunately, the Church is also in disarray at this time and is failing to give a healthy model of male leadership. Even at parish level many of the clergy exemplify the absentee father who puts the needs of others before the needs of his own family; yet St Paul clearly says, 'If anyone does not provide for his relatives, . . . [he] is worse than an unbeliever' (1 Tim. 5:8).

Our only hope is to go back to our foundation. We must take a fresh look at the one who models perfect fathering for us – God our Father.

4

THE PERFECT FATHER

'Lord, show us the Father and that will be enough for us.' (John 14:8)

Before we can hope to sort out the priorities and practices of a good father we first need a biblical revelation of God the Father. 'To know God as Father makes us different kinds of fathers, conditioned not just by our culture but by our experience of God.'[1] So wrote Tom Smail in his book on the often-forgotten member of the Godhead. Without such a revelation we are left to flounder around in a sea of differing opinions, outside pressures and personal prejudices. Some of these will be good, but many will lead us to repeat the mistakes of generations.

Imperfect ideas about God

Some people have formed impressions of God which fit their own preferences and prejudices, and these images have little biblical foundation. For example, there are those who envisage God as one who created the world and then left it to its own devices. Many would view fathering in those terms. Then there are people, similar to the fourth-century sect of the Hypsistarians who refused to worship God as Father but revered him only as the 'All Ruler and Highest',[2] for whom God is an authoritarian,

---

[1] Thomas A. Smail, *The Forgotten Father* (London: Hodder & Stoughton, 1980), p. 33.
[2] F. L. Cross (ed.), *The Oxford Dictionary of the Christian Church* (London: Oxford University Press, 1958), p. 673.

distant being who rules with a rod of iron and whose children can never enter into a loving relationship with him. Then there are the modern-day feminists who prefer to call God Mother and insist on him being referred to as She, even publishing their own prayers for liturgical worship to Mother God. These tend to give us a picture of God as a soft, effeminate type of Father or leave us with a void – no Father at all.

In all probability the above examples also reflect a personal experience of being fathered. We all have the tendency to project our limited understanding of fathering on to God the Father:

> There is obviously a very close psychological connection between our experiences of human fatherhood and our approach to God's fatherhood. The whole notion of fatherhood in whatever context it arises is highly emotive. It is surrounded by conscious memories, half-hidden loves, longings and resentments; you have only to speak for a few minutes to a group of ordinary people about God the Father to see that they are deeply involved in reactions that are at a far deeper level than the merely intellectual, and which say something about the homes in which they grew up and the presence or absence, in many different senses of those words, of their own fathers. Unless the whole image of fatherhood is corrected or even redeemed, we shall almost inevitably project onto God the father we have loved or missed, have desired or resented, so that our adult spiritual life will be secretly controlled by our reactions to our early family life.[1]

Some will have been privileged to relate to a good father. Even so, our experience will limit us to viewing fathering from the perspective of a fallen nature. In order to correct or redeem this image we should look more closely at the character of God the Father from the pages of scripture itself.

[1] Smail, *The Forgotten Father*, pp. 55–6.

God, the perfect Father

There is only one perfect Father, and that is God. He is
first of all seen as Father 'because he is the ultimate origin
of our being':[1] 'Have we not all one Father? Did not one
God create us?' (Mal. 2:10). The first man and woman
were created by him, and from them came the whole
human race. Although, as we shall see, God manifests
many motherly traits in his dealings with mankind, and is
sometimes likened to a mother in his care and tenderness
(Isa. 49:15), nevertheless, he relates to his people strongly
as a Father.

From the story of creation we understand that God is
in essence both male and female: 'So God created man
in his own image, in the image of God he created him;
male and female he created them' (Gen. 1:27). However,
he is never called 'mother', although he is referred to as
Father 15 times in the Old Testament and 245 times in the
New Testament.[2] Jesus, who related so intimately with his
heavenly Father, gives us the most insight into the paternal
nature of God. Hence the majority of references to God's
fathering come in the New Testament. Although the Old
Testament only infrequently refers to God as Father, it
nevertheless shows us very clearly the Father heart of God
through the history of his dealings with his people.

With so much material to select from, we cannot hope
to gain more than a glimpse of God's fathering in the Old
and New Testament. Just as a person who goes on holiday
is unable to record every experience he enjoyed, and only
has 'snapshot' impressions to share with those at home,
neither can we hope to give more than a few 'snapshots'.
Like a camera at a race meeting, we will proceed to take
a wide-angle view of the whole racecourse, but now and
again we will zoom in on one of the runners. In our case
this will be a facet of God's fathering in relationship to a
person or group of persons.

Let us deliberately lay aside our preconceived ideas of

[1] ibid., p. 33.
[2] ibid., p. 49.

a father before we begin. When our minds are filled with
our own ideas we have little space for new ones. Nor
does the truth find room in a mind full of misconceptions.
The experiences we had with our own fathers, even good
ones, will have been imperfect. The ideas and opinions of
others, even the most helpful, will be flawed. Only when
the perfect is in place will we have a plumb-line against
which to measure other ideas. Many of us tend to measure
our lives against how they look in comparison with other
people. In this way we soon get out of alignment. As
the Bible says: 'We all, like sheep, have gone astray'
(Isa. 53:6). It may seem logical to measure ourselves
against others, but the end result will be far from perfect.
Even a cursory look at God's perfect parenting should
challenge our inconsistencies and encourage us to make
any necessary alterations so that our family lives may more
perfectly reflect God's values.

The Father of Adam and Eve

'In the beginning God created the heavens and the earth'
(Gen. 1:1). In fact, he created a beautiful world in which
to place his first family. He showed his concern for Adam
by giving him a companion with whom to share his life,
and clear instructions for good living. He remained in
close contact with them, looking for them when he took
his evening walk in the garden. When they disobeyed his
instructions for life, he did not angrily destroy them but
spelled out the consequences of their actions. Even though
they had been deliberately disobedient and had incurred
his displeasure, he still continued to care for them. He
made them garments of skin and for their own good shut
them out of the garden which he had so lovingly created
for them. It must have broken his heart to have had the
whole creation marred by his very own children. Instead
of destroying them, however, he started a plan of action
which would save their future generations.

Yahweh-Elohim (Lord God)
God revealed himself to Adam and Eve by the double title
of 'Lord God' or 'Yahweh-Elohim'. Until Genesis 2:4 only
the name Elohim appears as a compound with the shorter
word 'El', and is derived from a root indicating strength
or might. Yahweh is the name of God most frequently
employed in the Old Testament, and in Genesis 2:4 it
appears for the first time in conjunction with Elohim. The
word Yahweh is thought to come from the root 'hwh' or
'hyh', which gives the idea of independent and underived
existence. When Moses was given this name from the
burning bush (Exod. 3:11–15), the flame that obtained
its sustenance from itself and not from its environment, it
was an impressive symbol of independent existence. The
name announced the faithfulness and unchangeableness of
God: 'I am that I am.'[1] When these two words, Yahweh
Elohim, are put together we obtain the impression of 'An
Ever-present, Strong, Deity'.

His presence gave man a sense of value
Because God was such a present, available, strong Father
to Adam and Eve, they were blessed with a sense of dignity
and worth. They had been made in God's own image and in
some way bore the family likeness. It is interesting to note
in families how much value a child derives from bearing a
family resemblance. When my eldest grandson was seven
he decided to write a book. His father had written a book,
and so too had his grandfather, and he wanted to be like
them. Another grandson was strutting round the house
recently with a toy ratchet in his hand. When asked what
he was doing, he replied, 'Fixin' things', which is exactly
what his Daddy does. Children receive a great deal of
kudos from being like a parent. Adam and Eve were
blessed with a sense of their own worth because they had
been made in the image of God.

[1] J. D. Douglas (ed.), *The New Bible Dictionary* (London:
Inter-Varsity Fellowship, 1962), p. 474.

His presence gave man a sense of achievement
They were also fortunate that their Father gave them a task which could provide them with a sense of achievement. God instructed them to rule over the fish, the birds and the other living creatures. He also placed them in the garden to work it and take care of it. Every person from the youngest to the oldest needs to know that his life has significance, and fathers can enhance or diminish their child's sense of significance by the sort of encouragement they give or the amount of time they allow their children to work alongside them.

When abroad recently, I was talking with a group of people about changing personal beliefs which may be causing them to be blocked in their growth as Christians. I gave some time for them to pray and think about their own misconceptions. Then I asked for anyone to share what God had shown him. A man put up his hand and said that his misconception was that if he wanted a job well done he had to do it himself. He felt God was telling him to let his children have a go at doing things, even if they made mistakes. God our Father gave us a wonderful example of how to give our children a sense of achievement and significance. One of the reasons that high unemployment is such a blight on a nation is that without work to do men and women begin to lose their sense of significance. Life often ceases to have meaning for such people.

His presence provided man with security
Lastly, Adam and Eve were secure in their relationship with their Creator. He had seen them take their first breath. He knew every bone in their bodies and had numbered the hairs on their heads. Not only was he responsible for forming them, but he obviously wanted the relationship to continue because he spent time with them, communicating with them and caring for them. At no time were they abandoned or ignored, as many children are by their earthly parents. Even when Adam and Eve had deliberately disobeyed him he still went on communicating with them.

One woman told me that when she was a small child her mother would punish her by not speaking to her. She said how much she had hated going to bed with the problem unresolved. Another lady said that her mother would sometimes not speak to her for days on end, not even to tell her what sin she had committed. Such parental silences can cause a child to feel desperately unloved and insecure.

Even though God never abandoned his wayward children and never ceased to communicate with them, they did to some extent forfeit the wonderful blessings which came directly from their close and unspoiled relationship with him. Suddenly the barrier of sin came down between Adam and Eve and their Creator, which immediately robbed them of those good feelings. Instead of possessing a sense of value because of being made in the image of God, they were covered in shame for having marred that image; they were left with an aching need to feel of value once again. Instead of a sense of achievement through their work, which would be natural and satisfying, they were shut out of the garden and were forced to toil with ground that was hard and unrewarding. The moment they disobeyed God their security was gone; they hid in fear from the one they had previously felt so close to. Their previously inherent blessings had become painful needs which, by and large, people have sought to meet unsuccessfully apart from God.

Every child born since that time has had a fundamental need for his father to provide him with those vital blessings. Some fathers succeed better than others in meeting these basic needs. When they do succeed, it puts a child in a good position later to receive them in full from their heavenly Father, who in the end is the only one who can truly meet them. But when an earthly father fails to pass on these blessings, a person may subsequently waste years trying to achieve them through his own efforts.

God's fathering of the children of Israel (Jer. 31:9)

Many generations passed after Adam and Eve and the consequences of the fall could be seen as man tried to meet his need to achieve, to be of value and to be safe apart from a relationship with his Creator. Eventually God's plan for saving and blessing his children began to take shape. He called Abram and said to him: 'I will make you into a great nation and I will bless you; I will make your name great, and you will be a blessing. I will bless those who bless you, and whoever curses you I will curse; and all peoples on earth will be blessed through you' (Gen. 12:2–3). But Abram and Sarai were childless, and although God reiterated his promise several times, Abram waited many years before Isaac was born. It was during the time of waiting that God revealed himself to Abram as 'God Almighty': 'When Abram was ninety-nine years old, the Lord appeared to him and said, "I am God Almighty; walk before me and be blameless. I will confirm my covenant between me and you and will greatly increase your numbers" ' (Gen. 17:1–2). This name, El Shaddai, gives us yet another insight into the Father heart of God.

El Shaddai (God Almighty)
Mighty to multiply. Although the meaning of El Shaddai is uncertain, it was used several times in conjunction with God's power to bless his children with fruitfulness (Gen. 17:1; 28:3; 35:11). Undoubtedly, under the name El Shaddai God showed himself to be sufficient and powerful enough to counter nature and cause the barren womb to conceive. At a conference in California recently, I watched a happy throng of some ten mothers queuing up to show the speaker their babies. The previous year, they had come to that conference barren and unable to conceive children. Our friend had prayed over these mothers and God had wonderfully answered these prayers and enabled them to conceive. Now they pushed forward with tears to show off their miracle babies.

Mighty to nurture. It is possible that the name El Shaddai could also be connected with another Hebrew word, *Shad*, which means breast. When Jacob was nearing the end of his life he pronounced a patriarchal blessing over his sons. When he came to Joseph he said: 'Joseph is a fruitful vine . . . because of your father's God, who helps you, because of the Almighty [El Shaddai], who blesses you with blessings of the heavens above, blessings of the deep that lies below, blessings of the breast [*Shad*] and womb . . .' (Gen. 49:22–5). At least one scholar, Nathan Stone, is convinced of the connection:

> *Shaddai* itself occurs forty-eight times in the Old Testament and is translated 'almighty.' The other word so like it, and from which we believe it to be derived, occurs twenty-four times and is translated 'breast.' As connected with the word *breast*, the title *Shaddai* signifies one who nourishes, supplies, satisfies. Connected with the word for God, *El*, it then becomes the 'One mighty to nourish, satisfy, supply.' Naturally with God the idea would be intensified, and it comes to mean the One who 'sheds forth' and 'pours' out sustenance and blessing. In this sense, then, God is the all-sufficient, the all-bountiful.[1]

The Mighty One of Jacob and the experience of being nursed at the breast is again linked in Isaiah: 'You will drink the milk of nations and be nursed at royal breasts. Then you will know that I, the Lord, am your Saviour, your Redeemer, the Mighty One of Jacob' (Isa. 60:16).

Thus the name teaches us several wonderful truths about God our Father. First, that God can meet us in our moments of complete helplessness. When Abram and Sarai were as weak as little children and incapable of making anything happen for themselves, God showed them his all-sufficient power. He said it clearly to Paul many thousands of years later, and he repeats it to us

[1] Nathan Stone, *Names of God* (Chicago: Moody Press, 1944), p. 34.

today: 'My grace is sufficient for you, for my power is made perfect in weakness' (2 Cor. 12:9).

Secondly, this title teaches us that Almighty God is directly associated with nourishment. He is able, like a mother, to nurture and provide abundantly for his children. He is the one who takes his children into his arms and gently sustains and comforts them. Once again this picture of God's capacity to mother us comes from Isaiah:

> 'Shout for joy, O heavens; rejoice, O earth; burst into song, O mountains! For the Lord comforts his people . . . Can a mother forget the baby at her breast and have no compassion on the child she has borne? Though she may forget, I will not forget you! See, I have engraved you on the palms of my hands . . .' (Isa. 49:13–16)

Yahweh-Jireh (The Lord will provide)

Abraham and Sarah eventually received their promised son. When Isaac was still a young boy, God tested his father's obedience and faith in his promises by ordering Abraham to sacrifice Isaac. Abraham reassured Isaac with the prophetically inspired words: 'God himself will provide the lamb for the burnt offering, my son' (Gen. 22:8). As we know, this was what God did in fact do. He stopped Abraham's hand just as he was about to kill Isaac and provided the offering himself, which inspired Abraham to call the place 'Yahweh-Jireh', the Lord will provide (Gen. 22:14).

God delights to provide for his children as a father. For many reasons an earthly father may fail in his task as provider, but God never fails. He is the Everlasting Provider. Especially has he provided for his children's greatest need, which is for a sacrificial lamb to take away the sin of the world. It was no coincidence that Mount Moriah, where God revealed himself as Provider, was the site of later Jerusalem, on which the Temple was built and where the substitutionary sacrifices were performed. It is the same mountain on which Jesus was put to death and became the Lamb of God who takes away the sin of the world.

He provides guidance. Isaac grew up and fathered Jacob, who in turn fathered twelve sons, who fathered the tribes of Israel. During the great famine they were forced to take up residence in Egypt, where their brother Joseph was already in a position of great authority. They multiplied in number, and in time became a threat to the Egyptians, who countered by making them slaves. But God did not forget his children, and eventually he put his rescue plan into operation. Through Moses, and with many miraculous signs, God brought the Israelites out of captivity and they began their journey through the wilderness. God did not rescue them and then leave them to negotiate the desert alone:

> By day the Lord went ahead of them in a pillar of cloud to guide them on their way and by night in a pillar of fire to give them light, so that they could travel by day or night. Neither the pillar of cloud by day nor the pillar of fire by night left its place in front of the people. (Exod. 13:21–2)

A true father is able to recognise difficult periods in his children's lives – desert experiences, when the strangeness of the situation renders a child helpless to cope on his own. A good father will make his child's need a priority at such a time, to be available to guide and light the way ahead. Our first child was three when number two was born, and I well remember David telling me that he felt he must make our eldest daughter, Charlotte, a priority at that time. I was recovering from the birth of the baby and was very caught up in trying to nurture a difficult feeder. So he took time off to be with Charlotte. Even as the baby grew older he made a point of taking Charlotte out visiting with him. This eased her transition from being an only child. She felt important being with her Daddy.

Rophe (The Lord who heals)

escape across the Red Sea was amazing, and
the people to fear the Lord 'and put their trust
in him and in Moses his servant' (Exod. 14:31). They
were so awed by their miraculous escape that Moses and
the people sang a song of triumph and praise to God. Then
Miriam, the prophetess, led the women in a dance. After
that wonderful mountain-top experience, one would have
thought the people of Israel would have learned to trust
in God's care of them for ever. But this was not to be.
Discomfort and pain cause all of us to grumble, and often
to lose sight of God's love. The people travelled for three
days in the desert and grew very thirsty. Eventually they
came to Marah, where they found water; but when they
tasted it, it was bitter. They started to complain. Even
so, God came to their rescue and turned the bitter water
sweet for them. At this point in their history God made
a decree for them: 'If you listen carefully to the voice of
the Lord your God and do what is right in his eyes, if you
pay attention to his commands and keep all his decrees,
I will not bring on you any of the diseases I brought on
the Egyptians, for I am the Lord, who heals you' (Exod.
15:26).

The word *rophe* appears some sixty or seventy times in
the Old Testament, always meaning to restore, to heal,
to cure, or a physician, not only in the physical sense but
in the moral and spiritual sense also. Out of Abraham's
trying experience on the mountain there had come a new
and comforting name of God, Yahweh-Jireh. Now out of
Israel's bitter experience in the wilderness there comes
another new and comforting name of God, Yahweh-
Rophe, Yahweh heals. And Yahweh here pledged himself on condition of their obedience to always be their
healer.[1]

He provides safe boundaries. Of all the people on the face
of the earth, God chose the Israelites to be his treasured
possession (Deut. 14:2). For him to put this condition of

[1] Stone, *Names of God*, p. 72.

obedience upon their health was a sign of his love rather than his desire to restrict their lives. His decrees, which he had yet to reveal to them in the ten commandments, were to be like signposts for healthy, fruitful living. He was giving them the benefit of his wisdom and knowledge. If they would follow these signposts, he would remain close to them and protect them from the ills that he had inflicted upon the Egyptians.

Every good father disciplines his children for their good. In this instance the disciplining first meant 'containment' – staying within certain boundaries. It was then extended to mean taking the consequences if those boundaries were violated. The consequences in turn would serve as a further means of discipline to cause the transgressors to move quickly back within the boundaries once again.

Enforcing good discipline is the mark of a caring Father. An absent, disinterested, or lazy parent leaves his children to their own devices. It takes time to explain the boundaries; it takes effort to enforce them and it takes wisdom to think up an appropriate consequence should the boundaries be deliberately breached. God was willing to enter into this type of time-consuming relationship with his children.

He relieves his children's suffering. Thus Yahweh-Rophe speaks to us of a God who cares enough to want his children to be healthy and who provides them with rules for healthy living. It also speaks of a Father who has the power to relieve his children's suffering.

The other day I witnessed a moving scene in our church. Halfway though the service a young girl crept in and took her seat beside her father and mother. She was in her teens and something had upset her. She sat down beside Dad and he put his arm around her. She laid her head on his shoulder and began to cry. He just stroked her hair as she wept. Gradually her sobs subsided and she began to relax. By the end of the service she was smiling. 'But I have stilled and quietened my soul; like a weaned child with its mother, like a weaned child is my soul within me. O Israel, put your hope in the Lord both now and for evermore' (Ps. 131:2–3).

God's fathering of King David

God knew him in his mother's womb and at his birth
'He said to me, "You are my Son; today I have become your Father" ' (Ps. 2:7). Whether King David was aware of the prophetic content of this psalm, we will never know. But there can be no doubt it also reflected his own relationship with God his Father. As a much loved son he knew that his Father had been concerned for him and watching over him even in his mother's womb; that he was present and actively involved in his birth; and that even when he was at his mother's breast he was there (Ps. 22:9–10).

God was there at a time when many fathers have opted out, assuming that 'It's a woman's world and men are best out of the way': 'From birth I was cast upon you' (v. 10). David knew his heavenly Father had been there at his birth and in the first moments of his life. As an adult he was able to look back and rejoice in that truth. Maybe David needed the healing which that knowledge brought him because his own father had not been present. In the past fathers were kept out of the delivery rooms, but policy has changed and today most hospitals recognise the importance of the father's presence. They are able to give their wives moral and physical support and encouragement. However, few people realise that the baby too needs support and encouragement during those hours of pain and fear.

Some babies suffer birth traumas that leave an indelible print on their lives. Many times I have witnessed remarkable healings from birth traumas when God has revealed the truth of his presence during that fearful experience. One woman had for many years suffered from claustrophobia without understanding the reason why. During a time of prayer God took her back to her birth and for a few moments she relived the panic of being held in the canal as her mother struggled to give her birth. God revealed his presence to her and she gradually grew calm. As the weeks progressed she realised that her claustrophobia had disappeared.

Certainly David found comfort in the knowledge that his heavenly Father was present with him from the moment of conception onwards.

A song-writer usually composes from his heart. His songs come out of his experience of life. Recently I learned a song, the words of which I found very moving. But they became even more special when I heard the experience which had inspired the words. The song speaks of God taking the precious from the worthless and giving beauty for ashes, love for hate. Then comes the statement: 'You are help to the helpless, strength to the stranger, and a father to the child that's left alone.'[1] Ordinary words! Until you realise that the man who wrote them was terribly abused by his father, was often shut in a cellar all day, and was eventually taken to hospital with limbs actually broken by the beatings of his cruel father. It was only when I heard that story that I realised how much the song reflected the healing that had taken place in the composer's life. He had obviously encountered the God who was able to be a 'Father to the fatherless' (Ps. 68:5).

David was special to God

King David also wrote songs which came from the heart and reflected the most important relationship of his life. His psalms give us wonderful glimpses of God's fathering. Only through the lips and life of Jesus do we get a fuller revelation. As we read these poems, which were usually written in the form of a prayer, we become aware that David felt very special to God and protected by him, and desired to stay in that protected place: 'Keep me as the

---

[1] Kevin Prosh and Tom Davis, Mercy Publishing, licence no. 753.

apple of your eye; hide me in the shadow of your wings',
he prays (Ps. 17:8).

David was protected by God
In other songs he described the gentler attributes of love
and compassion which he experienced in his relationship
with God (Pss. 23; 103). Yet in another we are brought
face to face with the protective strength of a Father who
is his son's refuge in times of trouble and a Rock on which
to build his whole life (Ps. 18:30–1).

David knew how so often earthly fathers fail their sons
and daughters. But he knew for sure that his heavenly
Father would always be there for him: 'Though my father
and mother forsake me, the Lord will receive me' (Ps.
27:10). The relationship David enjoyed with God his
Father was in fact central in his life:

> Yet I am always with you; you hold me by my right
> hand. You guide me with your counsel, and afterwards
> you will take me into glory. Whom have I in heaven but
> you? And earth has nothing I desire besides you. My
> flesh and my heart may fail, but God is the strength of
> my heart and my portion for ever. (Ps. 73:23–6)

God longs to father his children

Before we leave the Old Testament, it is worth mentioning
the cry of the prophets, who again and again call the children of Israel back to God, spelling out the consequences
of their rebellion and pleading with them on God's behalf
to repent. One of the most heart-rending pleas from God
comes through the prophet Jeremiah:

> '"I myself said, 'How gladly would I treat you like
> sons and give you a desirable land, the most beautiful
> inheritance of any nation.' I thought you would call me
> 'Father' and not turn away from following me. But like
> a woman unfaithful to her husband, so you have been
> unfaithful to me, O house of Israel," declares the Lord.'
> (Jer. 3:19–20)

God, the Father of Jesus

It is from the lips and life of Jesus, King David's greater
Son, that we gain the ultimate insight into the fatherhood
of God. 'The Christian norm of fatherhood and sonship is
the dealings between God and Jesus; the love with which
Jesus was loved and to which he trusted is the Father's
love and not any other . . .'[1] Through the gospels, and
in particular John's gospel, we are given many insights
into a divine relationship between a Father and a Son
which can be like no other in its perfection. Perhaps these
glimpses will spur us on to pursue a better way with our
own children.

God was involved in his birth
The important role fathers should play in their children's
lives is illustrated by the trouble God took to ensure that
his Son enjoyed the protection of an earthly father. In
fact God was intimately involved in the details of Jesus'
birth. It was carefully planned in heaven, and although the
coming of the Messiah was openly prophesied and looked
for, the details of the event were not plainly spelled out.
The Old Testament prophecies tended to be enigmatic,
which resulted in the actual birth of Christ being hidden
from the eyes of all but a few. Nevertheless, God could
not resist allowing one glorious outburst in song to blazon
the news of the Christ-child to a handful of shepherds. The
rest of the world slept on in ignorance of the momentous
happening in Bethlehem.

God watched over his childhood
Once born, Jesus was cared for by a loving human father
and mother, but at every turn his heavenly Father was
watching over him. He sent his messengers to help Joseph
do a good job of protecting the baby. We are told that 'the
child grew and became strong; he was filled with wisdom,
and the grace of God was upon him' (Luke 2:40). How

[1] Smail, *The Forgotten Father*, p. 56.

proud his heavenly Father must have been as he watched
his Son's progress. Physically, emotionally and spiritually
he was maturing, and God affirmed this process not with
money and material things, but by giving more of himself;
more of his grace. It was obvious that Jesus grew to love
his Father's presence. So much so that when he was twelve
years old and he had stayed behind in the Temple, he
replied to his parents' rebuke with a question: 'Didn't you
know I had to be in my Father's house?' (Luke 2:49). The
blessing of his Father rested fully upon Jesus as he grew to
manhood.

God blessed him with his Spirit, with affirmation, with encouragement

At the age of thirty, Jesus, along with many others, went
forward to be baptised by John. As John baptised Jesus,
God saw fit to draw attention to his beloved Son in two
significant ways. First he gave him the gift of his Spirit.
Then he publicly acknowledged his love for his son, and
encouraged him: 'You are my Son, whom I love; with
you I am well pleased' (Mark 1:11). The words bore no
relationship to achievement. Jesus had not yet started his
ministry. Such words put no pressure on the Son to win
his Father's approval. He already had that. They were
words that freed him to enjoy his Father's love for no
other reason than that he was owned as his Father's Son.
He was so sure of his Father's total acceptance of him that
later he was able to claim that God had placed his seal of
approval upon him (John 6:27).

Jesus enjoyed an open relationship with his Father

Jesus had the great privilege of knowing his Father well.
He said openly that the Father knew him and he knew
the Father (John 10:15). There was an enviable openness
between them. They were not afraid to be known by one
another. It is out of such open relationships that trust
grows, and it was a measure of that trust that God put
everything into the hands of Jesus (John 3:35). He showed
him what he was doing and shared many things with him

(John 5:20). Jesus could say: 'All that belongs to the Father is mine' (John 16:15). Jesus knew that his Father was always with him, and he continuously consulted with his Father so that they might be of one mind (John 8:29).

God delighted in his Son

Jesus lived his life to glorify his Father, and in total obedience to his Father's will he went to the cross; 'Therefore God exalted him to the highest place and gave him the name that is above every name, that at the name of Jesus every knee should bow' (Phil. 2:9–10). God was pleased to be called the Father of Jesus, and he truly delighted in his Son (Heb. 1:5). Finally, he received him back to heaven with a tremendous celebration (Ps. 24). There he is seated forever at the place of honour at his Father's right hand (Eph. 1:20).

We can learn from the way God the Father related to his Son. We can learn too from the way the Son related to his Father. As God's only Son he is of course unique, but in his incarnation he has become like one of us. His dependence upon his Father coincides in so many ways with the way we should and could relate.

Jesus responded with dependence and obedience

When any father gives himself generously to his son the response will nearly always be positive. Jesus responded to his Father with trust which showed itself in dependence and obedience. His dependence was not the sort that had grown out of insecurity, but sprang from a shared task and goal. It came from a oneness of heart and purpose: 'I and the Father are one' (John 10:30). Nor did his obedience spring from fear of failing or disappointing a perfectionist father; nor fear of displeasing an authoritarian father. Rather, it had grown out of an intimate relationship of love.

In fact, Jesus received his fullest satisfaction in doing his Father's will: 'My food is to do the will of him who sent me and to finish his work' (John 4:34). This delight in his Father's will was, however, put to the test in the

Garden of Gethsemane. The key to the final outcome was still the trust which had been built up over the thirty-three years of his human existence:

> The Father whom Jesus addresses in the garden is the one that he has known all his life and found to be bountiful in his provision, reliable in his promises and utterly faithful in his love. He can obey the will that sends him to the cross, with hope and expectation because it is the will of Abba whose love has been so proved that it can now be trusted so fully by being obeyed so completely.[1]

'Aloof, absent, and angry men have done much to give God a bad name through their distorted examples of fatherhood. As a result, the world is filled with broken children trapped in this awful deception, who are in desperate need of a true revelation of the Father heart of God.'[2] The Bible provides us with such a revelation. Even a cursory glance at it gives us a glimpse of God's fatherhood, which is so important for our understanding of what constitutes a good father and helps us in our need to be healed from the fatherless state in which so many of us have found ourselves. Within its pages we find a Father who desires a relationship with his children and who is continually concerned and involved in their well-being.

Human parenting leaves much to be desired when compared with God's parenting, and we could wallow in despair. But God encourages us to be like him; to be holy as he is holy (1 Pet. 1:16). He also sent his Holy Spirit to help us reach this goal. Therefore, as we move on to consider human fathering, we should bear in mind this image of perfect fathering and allow it to spur us on to become better parents.

[1] Smail, *The Forgotten Father*, p. 37.
[2] James Ryle, *The Hippo in the Garden* (Guildford: Highland Books, 1992), p. 50.

5

PRACTICAL FATHERING, 1:

MAKING A RELATIONSHIP

Many years ago I lived near a lady who was expecting her fifth child. I remember wondering how on earth she was going to cope with a small baby and four unruly children. Her husband never seemed to be at home, and when I asked she told me that he had a very important job and was a very busy man. Apparently, when she told him that number five was on the way he had responded that it was totally up to her. He just wanted her to understand that the children were her responsibility and that he would not be able to give her any help. I was shocked that any man could father a child and then opt out of caring for it except in a financial sense. I was thankful for my own husband's interest in his small daughter. Since that time I have periodically met other men who have stood apart from their families, believing that it was enough that they had a mother to look after them.

Mostly, however, a man is delighted when his wife becomes pregnant, and has a sense of pride in what they have achieved together. The thought of fatherhood is exciting yet awesome. 'Will I be a good father? Will I be able to earn enough to house and feed them?' These are the kind of thoughts that assail a first-time father-to-be. Occasionally a man can feel left out in the cold as his wife becomes more and more engrossed with her 'bump'. He may perceive the coming baby as a 'rival' for his wife's affections. These feelings may surface when the need to be mothered as a child has not been adequately satisfied. A man often looks to his wife to meet those needs, and the coming baby threatens the attention that he has grown accustomed to receiving. This may account for some men's anger towards their offspring, and in some cases this is expressed in real cruelty. Sometimes these emotions are only fleetingly present and pose no real problem. However, when they continue to plague a man it is time to seek some help before it affects the quality of fathering a son or daughter could receive.

My friend's husband may have considered himself excused from any intimate contact with his children by reason of his work or temperament. But nothing should in fact exempt a man from being a father to his offspring, because no one can replace him. His wife may be a 'superwoman' or an 'earthmother', but she is a woman and therefore a mother, and can never become a father. She offers a rich variety of care. She nurtures, comforts, and provides the home with a warmth a father would find difficult to supply. A father, on the other hand, normally sets the boundaries around the home; offers the protection the family needs; provides for them materially and gives the encouragement and affirmation which are vital to his children's sense of self-worth. If a man could comprehend the length, breadth and depth of fatherhood, he would have only one feeling – awe! It is an awesome task to be a father.

Without a father the children will grow up with a gap in their experience of parenthood. In some cases the gap is partially filled by a grandfather, uncle or some other male relation. Elyce Wakerman, researching father loss, discovered that the women in her study were surprisingly indifferent towards, and unaffected by, men who acted as surrogates – except in the case of grandfathers! 'Alone among surrogate fathers, these men were able to make a positive contribution to their father-absent granddaughters' lives, helping them to feel more confident and assertive than fatherless women whose grandfathers did not participate in their upbringing.'[1] Grandfather or no, unless there is a good gap-filler a child without a father will enter adulthood with a degree of emotional handicap.

Values

It was the one-time church growth consultant, John Wimber, who introduced us to the concept of setting values in our lives. Values are rather like the foundations of a building. The stronger they are, the bigger and better the building that can be built on top of them. Out of our values come our priorities, and out of our priorities come our practices. In other words, if you agree wholeheartedly with a certain value you will prioritise it in some way. Perhaps by putting it in your diary and setting aside time to do something about it. Then you will actually put into practice what you have planned. If you never actually get around to putting it into practice, then in fact that value is not really as high on the list as you thought it was.

Although David and I had never articulated our values, on hearing John talk we realised that we had held some strong values when bringing up our four children. I recently asked David what those had been for him as a father. His reply was that he valued his relationship with the girls and he valued their physical, emotional, mental and spiritual growth.

We should remind ourselves how much God valued his relationship with his children and how he continually concerned himself with their well-being. With the example of God's perfect fathering in mind, let us examine, in this chapter and the next, two facets of practical fathering: (1) the relationship a father enjoys with his children, and (2) the physical, mental, emotional and spiritual growth of each child.

---

[1] Elyce Wakerman, *Father Loss* (London: Piatkus, 1986), p. 53.

The relationship

If a father values his relationship with his children, he has to make it a priority to relate daily to them in some meaningful way. The practical outworking of this will be through communication. He will communicate with them as often as he can, using all the means available to him.

Consistent communication

We know a couple who live nearby with a new baby. When we were passing their house shortly after the birth, the father, beaming with pride, came to the gate to describe his baby son. Knowing that I had written about families, he asked me politely what advice I had for him. 'Start communicating with your son now,' I said. 'And don't let anything stop you as long as you both live.' Good communication is becoming a rare experience in most families. As I have already said, the average father spends three minutes a day talking to his son or daughter, who spends about three hours a day in front of the TV. One could ask who has the greatest impact upon those children – the media or the parents? Besides which, the television is often a solitary occupation.

In this technological age of microwave ovens, deep freezers and prepacked meals, many families find it easier to eat separately and at times which are most convenient to each individual member. So what in the past has been the traditional place for family discussion is gradually disappearing in favour of convenience.

Recently a depressed teenager complained to me that she never had any chance to talk to her parents. 'Why not talk to them at meal times?' I asked, quite expecting her reply to be that she didn't know where to begin. Instead she gave a short laugh and said, 'Meal times! We never sit down to meals together. Mum keeps the fridge full of grub and we eat whenever we feel like it. I usually take my meals up to my room.'

Even though our instant, technological and individualistic society has lost some of the old venues for communicating, it does not diminish its importance. The answer is not to bemoan the fact that they have gone, but to search for ways of communicating which fit more appropriately into the world in which we find ourselves.

Start early
It is never too early to start finding opportunities to get to know one's child. Many a man feels that once his wife becomes pregnant he is on the sidelines until the birth, when he will be needed to drive his wife into hospital. It may seem that way because a woman appears to be the major participator in the birthing process; nevertheless, a father should be actively involved in his child's life from the moment of conception onwards. Whenever a couple tell me they are expecting a baby, I encourage the father to talk to the baby while it is in the womb. It is a golden opportunity for them to get acquainted. Dr Thomas Verney would encourage this prenatal, paternal bonding:

> A child hears his father's voice in utero, and there is solid evidence that hearing that voice makes a big emotional difference. In cases where a man talked to his child in utero using short soothing words, the newborn was able to pick out his father's voice in a room even in the first hour or two of life. More than pick it out, he responds to it emotionally. If he's crying, for instance, he'll stop. That familiar soothing sound tells him he is safe.[1]

I have told the story elsewhere of how my son-in-law Chris got to know his first baby. He used to sit next to his wife during the pregnancy and place his hands on her bump and talk to it. As he did this every evening they began to notice that the baby was responding by moving over in the womb and nestling close into his father's hand.

[1] Thomas Verney with John Kelly, *The Secret Life of the Unborn Child* (New York: Dell, 1981), p. 31.

When a father has communicated regularly with his baby in the womb he is in an ideal position not only to be present for his wife during the labour, but also for his baby. Of all the experiences in a child's life birth is probably the most catastrophic: 'Even in the best of circumstances, birth reverberates through the child's body like a seismic shock of earthquake proportions.'[1] If a baby already knows his father's voice, then he will be encouraged and comforted by hearing it when he is being pushed and squeezed out of his warm, safe haven in the womb.

To watch a mother with her new baby is always a very moving experience, but it is equally touching to see the pride on a father's face as he holds his tiny son in his arms or the tenderness with which he rocks his little girl. In the majority of instances compassion and protectiveness are all there within the male breast. All that is needed is the understanding that the man has a valuable and unique contribution to make to his child's life. He should allow no one to rob his child of the immense privilege of communicating intimately and meaningfully with a physically and emotionally present father right from the start.

> Given a chance, a man can be just as 'motherly' as a woman; protective, giving, stimulating, responsive to his children's needs, caring. Largely because the stereotypes and misunderstandings about fathers run so deep in our culture, it has taken us an inordinately long time to notice these simple facts of life. Even people who should have known better often did not. Anthropologist Margaret Mead was probably being ironic when she defined a father as a biological necessity before birth and a social accident after it, but she was also expressing a widely held view.[2]

[1] Verney, *The Secret Life of the Unborn Child*, p. 98.
[2] ibid., p. 158.

Keep going

As a child grows older, communication becomes harder for the father. He is often out most of the day, and the child is already in bed when he gets home. But no father can afford to have gaps in the relationship. As a child passes through the developmental stages of childhood he is dependent on both a mother and a father to see him successfully through those stages. Some of the tasks of childhood are best accomplished with mother in attendance, and others with father. Yet others are only successfully achieved with the help of both parents. As we look more closely at the growth of the child we shall see the importance of a father's presence at different stages.

Communication is particularly difficult for men who were solitary children, or who were taught to suppress their feelings, or whose fathers did not communicate with them or who were sent away to boarding school at a young age. As I have described earlier, such men have no model for relating intimately with their children. Unless they want their children to grow up at an emotional distance from them, and with problems that belong especially to the fatherless, they will have to change. Change is only implemented in a person's life when there is good motivation. We are all too cowardly and lazy to make changes unless there is a good pay-off. The dividend in this instance is well worth the effort: an open, trusting relationship with a child who looks to you for support and guidance, and who is growing up to be healthy in every way.

How, then, does a father practically work out this relationship?

Through play

When a father and a child of whatever age play together, communication takes place at several levels and with great ease and enjoyment. The psychologist and writer Dr James Dobson had one son whom he put to bed every night when he was small, 'and we laughed and we played and we talked about Jesus. I would hide his sister's stuffed animals around the house, and then we would turn out the lights and hunt them with flashlights and a toy rifle. He never tired of that simple game.'[1] A rough-and-tumble with a son involves closeness, healthy touch, laughter, talk and time. Playing piggy-back rides with a little girl involves the same variety of communication. Plenty of opportunity for appropriate touch is important for a child's development. The world-renowned family therapist Virginia Satir used to say that all people need four hugs a day just for 'maintenance'.[2] So for 'development' a child must need many more.

For the older child, playing either a ball game or an indoor game with Dad can be the highlight of the week or the holiday. No family game in our house was ever worth playing unless Daddy joined in. No film was worth watching unless he was going to watch too. No outing was much fun unless he shared it. Saturday was our day off when we lived in Chile. In the winter we would often go and play in the grounds of an old colonial house which had been converted into a museum. The 'Parque Vergara' was large and full of exotic plants and giant trees. Daddy would become the hunter and everyone else had to hide. The aim was to reach 'home base' without being caught. As the hunter, David was tireless and merciless. The park would soon be filled with the screams of excited children. Twenty-five years later, when I watch my grandsons playing with their fathers I see that a father's magic is as strong as ever.

The writer Catherine Marshall remembers her father constructing an outsize sandbox for her, a see-saw which was sturdier and longer than any to be found in the shop, and a wonderful swing. They would also play indoor games, all of which revolved around her father: 'What was pure gold were the hours he spent with us

[1] Rolf Zettersten, *Dr. Dobson: Turning Hearts Toward Home* (Dallas: Word, 1989), p. 2.
[2] D. Charles Williams, *Forever a Father* (Wheaton, Ill.: Victor Books, 1991), p. 13.

children playing Parcheesi, caroms, checkers, dominos, Rook, Old Maid, jackstraws, jacks or putting together countless jigsaw puzzles.'[1]

Through work

Not only did Catherine's father play with her, he also allowed her to spend time with him when he was working. Sometimes it was to run an errand with him or to visit some parishioners or just be with him while he did repairs around the house. There are many chores around the house and garden which can be shared with a child. Few children will refuse an opportunity of spending time with Dad, and working together with him builds up a child's feeling of significance. The advantage of spending time on a mundane task is the opportunity it gives for sharing together. There is a myth about

> which implies that the amount of time spent together is not as significant as the quality of time experienced . . . The reality of the matter is that any moment can be transformed into quality time if a parent is alert, tuned in, and responsive. Quality and quantity are necessary. Children need a lot of time to hang out, run errands, participate in chores, have fun, or just talk. The truth is that quality time often comes during quantity times . . . The 'one-minute father' will have trouble accomplishing this kind of quality without investing quantity time.[2]

When a child is working or having fun with Dad, there is the opportunity for a father to listen to his child and to understand him better. A father needs to attune himself to his children. Eric Rayner, a psychologist and researcher, is convinced that men are mistaken when they assume that they can safely ignore their children in early infancy:

> A father who has mingled with his children from

[1] Catherine Marshall, *Meeting God at Every Turn* (London: Hodder & Stoughton, 1981), p. 23.
[2] Williams, *Forever a Father*, p. 30.

babyhood will not only have the pleasure of seeing and contributing to their growth, but will also know them intimately in all their non-verbal idiosyncrasies. Only when he intuitively knows their modes of thought will he be able to be a teacher when the time comes to impart new knowledge.[1]

For most children, the only opportunity they have to work alongside their fathers is doing household chores. Few children have the opportunity of visiting and understanding their father's work-place. When a man is self-employed or working from home his children are more able to visit their father's work and are able then to picture him and what he is doing when they are apart. Generally, a father spends such a large slice of his life in some mysterious office or factory that a child can feel totally cut off from a huge chunk of his father's life.

One man whose father was emotionally distant from him said that he used to watch for any clue as to what it might be like to be a man. He used to watch his father do male things like shaving. He wanted to know what it felt like to be a proper, real man with a suit on who had customers and went to work. He felt that the world of men was somewhere else – hidden. He desperately wanted to be the other side of that curtain. His father never bridged that gap for him, and all his life he felt that something masculine had been left out of him. Just by talking to a child about his work, or showing him pictures of what he does, a father could help a child to break through the barrier. Sometimes it is even possible to take a child to visit the work-place and introduce him to the world outside, where Daddy lives most of his life. One of my sons-in-law is a clergyman, and he regularly involves his boys in church activities. From the age of five they have assisted Dad at weddings and baptisms, and have attended Compline with him.

As we have already stated, not all communication is

[1] Eric Rayner, *Human Development* (London: Allen & Unwin, 1986), p. 218.

verbal, and especially when passing on important values for life one method of doing so is especially powerful.

Through example

Whether we like it or not, parents are an example to their children. To their sons, fathers are a model of manhood, fatherhood and how to be a husband. To their daughters, mothers model womanhood, motherhood and being a wife. The young of every species learn from their elders, and humans are no exception. Teaching is happening constantly throughout childhood, both formally and informally. It is often the informal teaching which has the most profound effect on a child. In other words, what a child receives through his senses tends to penetrate to the deepest level. For example, when a tired child comes in from school and opens the front door to the smell of rock-buns cooking and the sound of mother singing, and then receives a hug, that child may never receive any formal teaching about motherhood but has in fact received, quite informally, teaching which will never be forgotten.

Adolescent boys in particular need a good role model. They are going through a transitional period which can be very confusing. They look around at this time for a hero who attracts them enough to copy. If Dad is available and sufficiently attractive, he will be chosen. But if he is unapproachable, unreliable, uninterested or too busy, then he disqualifies himself. The boy automatically looks around for another champion on whom to base his emerging identity. He could easily choose someone quite unsuitable.

On the other hand, Dad may be the one whose lifestyle is unsuitable, but because he is 'My dad' he becomes the chosen hero. An unknown author wrote the following words to fathers who had the privilege of raising sons:

'Well, what are you going to be, my boy, when you have
reached manhood's years – a doctor, a lawyer, or actor
great, moving throngs to laughter and tears?'
But he shook his head as he gave reply, in a serious

way that he had: 'I don't think I'd care to be any of them – I want to be just like my Dad!'

He wants to be like his dad! You men, did you ever think, as you pause, that the boy who watches your every move is building a set of laws. He's molding a life you're the model for; and whether it's good or bad depends on the kind of example set to the boy who'd be like his dad.

Would you have him go everywhere you go? Have him do just the things you do? And see everything that your eyes behold, and woo all the gods you woo? When you see the worship that shines in the eyes of your lovable little lad, could you be content if he gets his wish, and grows up like his dad?

It's a job that none but yourself can fill; it's a charge you must answer for; it's a duty to show him the road to tread ere he reaches manhood's door. It's a debt you owe for the greatest joy on this old earth to be had – the pleasure of having a boy to raise, who wants to be just like his dad![1]

The sort of fathering we are describing takes time and effort. Most children are more accustomed to having what the psychologist Charles Williams calls an 'instant Father':

The instant father is one that is born out of the fast-paced society we live in today . . . An instant father blasts in after a long day and acts as if he and his son are emotionally close even if they really are not. There is an all-glitter-but-no-gold feeling within the son about the relationship as Dad says, 'Hey, son, how are you doing?' gives a quick hug and continues, 'You're great, gotta go,' leaving his child once again. Boys whose fathers regularly enter and leave their lives have an illusion of time together, but feel cheated,

[1] Herbert V. Prochnow and Herbert V. Prochnow, Jr, *Jokes, Quotes and One-Liners* (Wellingborough: Thorsons Publishing Group, 1987), p. 412.

frustrated, unfulfilled, yearning for more of Dad's time. Ironically the sons themselves often feel guilty for the lack of appreciation they show towards their dads and the little bit of quality time they have received.[1]

However, a father who values the relationship and makes it a priority in his life and then practises it through communication leaves his children with an inheritance they will never exhaust. Out of the relationship grows trust, and trust is the best soil in which to grow children.

[1] Williams, *Forever a Father*, p. 30.

6

PRACTICAL FATHERING, 2:

A CHILD'S GROWTH

Two of our grandchildren have just started to walk. I had forgotten the excitement that particular feat engenders. It is as if no child had ever walked before! Watching a child grow and mature is a most satisfying experience. Sadly, many children grow-up physically and mentally but remain stunted in other important areas of life. For the growth to be healthy and balanced a child needs help; he needs this help from two separate people who are significantly different. So often a father thinks that growth is a mother's concern, and may never have stopped to ask himself what part he should be playing in his child's maturing process.

Physical growth

A child's mental and physical development usually give parents most concern, and these are the areas over which they seem to have the least power. But they do have some influence and can certainly help or hinder a child's progress in these areas.

It is normally the father who provides the resources to keep a family housed and fed. In these days of high unemployment many fathers are concerned lest they are unable to accomplish such tasks adequately. Providing a child can be kept warm and has good, if plain food, missing out on the luxuries will do no harm. We sometimes forget that during the last war food and fuel were very scarce. Most families did without any luxuries and survived on the bare necessities. Although there was much physical and emotional suffering during those years, the health of the nation did not appear to suffer in a significant manner. This is not to say that we should be satisfied with such a low level of existence for anyone. It is just to say that simple fare is not necessarily harmful.

There are other kinds of provision, however, which enhance physical health and need to be consistently supplied by parents. Physical health not only depends on food and warmth, but also on exercise and safety. Fifty years ago, winter and summer, children would regularly walk or cycle to school. In these days school is reached either by bus or car, or it is just around the corner. Fathers usually play more energetically than mothers, and children need the exercise that ball games, cycle rides and runs give them. Games also provide practice in winning and losing, which are important lessons to learn.

Protection is another aspect of physical maturity. A child who has not learned safety rules may harm himself. A wise parent will set a good example in this respect. When we lived in Chile we suffered a number of severe earthquakes. Because these were frequent occurrences we tried to prepare the children for them. Obedience was of utmost importance, and I would explain that obedience could be a matter of life or death. One of the problems in a quake is falling debris. Our house proved to have a tendency to shed its ceilings, even in quite small quakes, so we had some simple rules for protection. During the night, the moment the house began to rock each child was to crawl under her bed, and during the day she should stand in a doorway. One night we woke to the sound of rumbling and found the house was shaking in a frightening manner. We called out immediately: 'Under the beds.' Each child obeyed without a murmur. David and I found ourselves the only ones unable to reach that safe position. We had failed to remember that our bed had a frame which almost touched the floor and we were left with heads under the bed and the rest of our bodies sticking up in a rather undignified manner.

Our example on that night did nothing to benefit the children!

By and large the girls were obedient to the rules we imposed. Only years after the experience did David and I learn of one nasty accident which taught them a sharp lesson in obedience. Near our house we had a railway line with a main road running alongside it. The other side of both was a little kiosk which sold sticky sweets. The girls loved to spend their pocket-money at the kiosk, but to do so they had to take a long route via the crossing which was governed by lights. To cross nearer to the house was quicker, and popular with all the neighbours, but very dangerous. And rules were rules! At least they were until one day when laziness and insubordination won the day. 'Nothing is coming, and who will ever know?' they thought. So they began to cross the line. Half-way across they heard the hoot of the train, and around the corner it appeared. They began to jump over the lines at speed, but Tasha, the youngest, lost her footing and fell. They told us later it was the worst moment of their lives. The rest of them grabbed her hands and dragged her to safety just in time. Thankfully they learned a lesson in obedience without coming to any more harm than a few scratches and bruises.

David was certainly perceived as the authority figure in our household, and the children respected his discipline. This did not mean I, as mother, had no say in setting the boundaries for the family. In fact we shared many of the tasks of parenting, but functionally David was the leader. He was physically and emotionally more fitted for this task. Being physically weaker and emotionally softer, I enjoyed the more caring aspect of mothering. St Paul seems to indicate that the father should be the person with ultimate authority. Writing about overseers in the church, he says that they must be men who can manage their own family: 'If anyone does not know how to manage his own family, how can he take care of God's church?' (1 Tim. 3:5). And writing about fathering to the Ephesian church, he says: 'Fathers, do not exasperate your children;

instead, bring them up in the training and instruction of the Lord' (Eph. 6:4).

A man does not have to be dominant or aggressive to be the leader. He needs to be strong and firm, which gives a child a sense of safety. This means he can relax and enjoy the excitement of living in a daily expanding world. Researchers Westley and Epstein studied a group of college students who showed unusual emotional health. They found that 'regarding the issue of power, the healthiest families were found to be father-led. Next most healthy were those which were father-dominant, next egalitarian and worst mother-dominant.'[1]

Mental growth

This is one area of development which some may think can be left to the educational authorities. Although some children are born with higher IQs than others, nevertheless parents have the ability to frustrate or assist their child's mental development – especially the father. Another researcher, Dr Martin Deutsch, 'found that the father's presence and conversation – especially at dinner time – stimulates a child to perform better at school'.[2] Dr Armand Nicli, in his White House paper (25 October 1984), 'found that an emotionally or physically absent father contributes to a child's (1) low motivation for achievement; (2) inability to defer immediate gratification for later rewards; (3) low self-esteem; and (4) susceptibility to group influence and to juvenile delinquency'.[3]

Winston Churchill, though obviously intelligent, performed very poorly both at his prep-school and at Harrow. Writing of those early years, his son Randolph throws some light on the possible reasons for his poor performance:

[1] Robin Skynner, *Explorations with Families* (London: Methuen, 1987), p. 295.
[2] Josh McDowell and Dr Norm Wakefield, *The Dad Difference* (San Bernardino: Here's Life Publishers, 1989), p. 11.
[3] ibid.

The neglect and lack of interest in him shown by his parents were remarkable, even judged by the standards of late Victorian and Edwardian days. Winston's letters to his mother from his various schools abound in pathetic requests for letters and for visits . . . Lord Randolph was a busy politician with his whole interest absorbed in politics.[1]

Young Winston even wrote begging his father to visit him:

You have never been to see me & so everything will be new to you. Ducker is reserved specially for the visitor to look at. You will see the Vaughan Library – the Gymnasium – the Racquet Courts – My room – & other places. Am going to school this morning, so I must say 'Good Bye' & Love and Kisses
Remain Your loving son
Winston S. Churchill
P.S. I shall be awfully disappointed if you don't come.

'"Do try and get Papa to come", he wrote to his mother. "He has never been." But Lord Randolph did not go.'[2] Dr Welldon, the headmaster, had to drop some hints to the effect 'that it might "perhaps not be disagreeable" to him and to Lady Randolph to come some time in the summer and take "at least the opportunity of seeing what Winston's school life is like"'.[3] In fact Winston had been at Harrow for eighteen months before his father first visited him there.

This experience was hardly unique to Winston Churchill. It is interesting that nearly forty years later he was to write in his Life of Marlborough that 'famous men are usually the product of an unhappy childhood'. And 'in 1898 he wrote of the Mahdi: "Solitary trees, if they grow

[1] Randolph S. Churchill, *Winston S. Churchill, Youth 1874–1900* (London: Heinemann, 1966), p. 45.
[2] ibid., p. 125.
[3] ibid., p. 123.

at all, grow strong; and a boy deprived of a father's care often develops, if he escapes the perils of youth, an independence and vigour of thought which may restore in after life the heavy loss of early days.' "[1]

It would seem that in some homes today the father's only input to his child's mental development is actually to thwart the process. He shows little interest in the child until .parents' evening at school, and then will react strongly to the concerns of the teacher and proceed to criticise the child for not having done better. One survey showed that on average a child receives ten negative comments from his parent to one positive comment, and yet experts in the field of child psychology say that it takes about four positive comments to offset the damage to self-esteem made by one negative comment.[2]

A parent criticises a child to improve his performance. Unfortunately, it usually has the opposite effect and instead inhibits the child by robbing him of his self-confidence. Encouragement is the fertiliser for mental growth. In fact it is for any type of performance. Not long ago I heard a friend from the USA tell a story which underlined the vital role encouragement plays in a child's development. When my friend was about four or five years old he lived on his grandfather's farm in Northern Minnesota. One day his grandfather sat him on one of the old cart horses. The little boy straddled the huge animal and his grandfather led him around the field. After a while the grandfather looked up at him proudly and said: 'Kenny boy, you're a natural.' From that moment on the boy believed he was a natural rider. He never mounted a horse again until he was twenty-one. He was in the army and had entered the US Modern Pentathlon, in which one of the events is equestrian jumping. Undaunted by his lack of experience, he began training, and in 1968 in Mexico City won the riding event. He was not too surprised at his success, because, after all, he was a 'natural'!

[1] ibid., p. 241.
[2] McDowell and Wakefield, *The Dad Difference*, p. 25.

Children listen for the masculine voice of affirmation. Sadly, some keep listening for it and never hear it because it never comes. There is nothing that warms the heart of a child quite like praise from Daddy. The author Elyce Wakerman, who lost her father at the age of three, says she still catches herself wondering as she draws to the end of a chapter: 'Daddy, are you clapping?'[1] A child needs encouragement from both his father and mother, but especially from father. Mummy is normally encouraging, and her smile always brings a sense of well-being to a child. But to win Daddy's approval, to see his smile of pride, can build up a child's sense of significance and self-worth – just as his disapproval can easily rob him of those important and necessary feelings.

I remember our own children's reactions to Dad's criticism. If David ever commented negatively on a project of theirs, my positive words never seemed to outweigh his criticism. He had a far better eye for detail than me, and he had the irritating habit of seeing the one flaw or mistake, which I had missed. There was one occasion, which David still remembers with regret, when our youngest was making her first blouse. Finding sewing so difficult myself, I was thrilled that she had nearly finished it and I praised her highly. However, David's quick eye noticed a major flaw in the blouse. He thought that by pointing it out he was helping her and she would be able to put it right. Tasha's reaction was quickly to lose interest in the enterprise, and she never finished it.

It is not easy to be a good father! But it is worth remembering that encouragement must come before criticism, and that when criticism is necessary it should be introduced as subtly as possible. This David managed to do on another occasion. Our eldest daughter had crocheted a very holey and indecent mini-skirt for herself. She proudly showed it off to her father, who was very complimentary about her effort. Then he diplomatically suggested that a lining for

[1] Elyce Wakerman, *Father Loss* (London: Piatkus, 1986), p. 273.

the skirt would add a finishing touch. Basking in the affirmation, she was happy to comply with his suggestion.

Emotional growth

Not long ago I met a young doctor. He was physically and mentally mature but talked about a problem with homosexuality. His father had died just after he was born. He was his mother's only child, so they had been very close to one another. The lack of a father had handicapped him quite severely in his emotional growth.

Normally a child needs a physically present and emotionally available father figure if he is to grow up to be healthy. In the early weeks his presence is needed more for protection than anything else. The receiving of nurture is the main task, and this can be difficult when there are too many disturbances. Therefore father is required to protect mother and baby so that this process may carry on uninterrupted. Also, Dad is required to give Mum a break now and again. I remember feeling so grateful when David would pace the floor with one or other of his tiny daughters, singing psalms and canticles until she fell asleep! Nor should being a man exempt him from some of the more 'motherly' chores. Changing nappies, bathing and later feeding his child can all be part of relationship-building for a father. As this relationship forms, so too does a child's sense of worth and self-esteem.

At first a mother enters into a state of symbiosis with the child. The child psychologist D. W. Winnicott calls this a state of 'Primary Maternal Preoccupation'. As the child grows a gradual separation should take place. But mothers need help to draw away from the original closeness. In many homes the father is absent for reasons of work or because he is thought to be of no account and therefore does nothing to help the process. 'An emotionally distant male is a necessary precondition for the perpetuation of an intense mother-child relationship.'[1] This was the problem

[1] Edwin H. Friedman, *Generation to Generation* (London: The Guilford Press, 1985), p. 105.

for my doctor friend. He had had no father to prevent him continuing too long in an intense relationship with his mother.

A mother is a mother all her life, and her desire to protect and comfort her children is natural. This is often expressed through an attempt to control them, even when they are adults. When father has not been available to interrupt the closeness between mother and child, this control can have a detrimental effect. It is vitally important for both a daughter and a son to separate in a healthy and appropriate way from their mother. In order for a father to interrupt the closeness between a mother and child he first of all needs to be present. This task is not achieved from a distance. Then he needs to become an important part of his child's life. At the same time the intimacy between himself and his wife needs to be maintained and strengthened. The child must become aware of the closeness which exists between his mother and father, and know that their love is different from the one which exists between himself and his parents. It is particularly important for the boy to make this separation, because if he remains trapped by the feminine he is in dire trouble. He may not necessarily suffer from a sexual neurosis, but, as many wives will testify, he may be dominated by his mother all his life and not be able to give himself properly to his wife and family.

Jesus was a good example of an emotionally secure person who was sure of his autonomy and separateness from his mother. He honoured his mother and yet would not allow her to control him. On several occasions she tried to do so, but he firmly stated his position. At the wedding at Cana in Galilee, when they ran out of wine Mary tried to involve Jesus. He spoke quite sternly to her: 'Woman, what have I to do with thee? Mine hour is not yet come' (John 2:4, KJV). Another time when he was surrounded by needy people, his family came looking for him to take charge of him. They said: 'He is out of his mind' (Mark 3:21). But Jesus quickly made his position clear. '"Who are my mother and my brothers?" he asked. Then he looked at those seated in a circle around him and said, "Here are my mother and my brothers! Whoever does God's will is my brother and sister and mother"' (Mark 3:33–5). With these words he made it quite clear that his family, and in particular his mother, could not control him. However, when he hung dying upon the cross his mother's welfare concerned him and he committed her to the care of John, the disciple whom he loved (John 19:26–7). To separate from one's mother is vital for emotional wholeness, but this does not mean that one ceases to honour her.

Father is needed to help with the necessary separation from mother, but also to enable a proper differentiation of the sexes. Between the age of three and four years the sexual identity should be decided and a boy, for example, will know that he belongs on Daddy's side of the line; the opposite to his mother. A little girl will know she is on her mother's side; the opposite to her father. Robin Skynner put it so aptly when he said that a child needs two landmarks to get his bearing sexually and find out where he is – and he needs them to be a certain distance apart.[1] Of course Dad is not only sexually different, he is different in many exciting ways. He feels different, he smells different, he sounds different and he stands for different things. Mother is there most of the time, but Dad tends to come and go. He becomes the prime representative of the outside world and forms a bridge to that world beyond the nursery which is exciting and mysterious.

Fathering a daughter and fathering a son have many common factors, but some tasks are different. For a son, a father should be a promise of the manhood to come, an initiator into that manhood, and also a model of it. Beginning at age three and continuing throughout childhood a boy is searching deeply for a masculine model on which to

[1] Robin Skynner and John Cleese, *Families and How to Survive Them* (London: Methuen, 1983), p. 247.

build his sense of self.[1] For this reason a father should be available to his sons, relating to them and speaking often about becoming men, preparing them for their future role. As he talks about it he will be modelling masculinity, as well as the tasks of husbanding and fathering to them. They are then left in no doubt who they are and where they belong. One of my grandsons, aged five, recently explained to me that one day his voice will break. 'It will go deep and be like my daddy's,' he said. 'Then what will you do?' I asked him. With a smile of anticipation he replied: 'Then I will be a preacher like daddy.' He had obviously been having a heart to heart with his father!

The Harvard psychologist Samuel Osherson writes: 'What does it mean to be male? If father is not there to provide a confident, rich model of manhood, then the boy is left in a vulnerable position; having to distance himself from mother without a clear and understandable model of male gender upon which to base his emerging identity.'[2]

Not only does he need to receive a good model of masculinity, he also needs to be 'called out' into manhood when the proper time comes. Some cultures still hold initiation ceremonies, when boys are initiated into manhood by the elders of the village or tribe. Writing on what it means to be male, Robert Bly explains that only men can initiate men, as only women can initiate women: 'Women can change the embryo to a boy, but only men can change the boy to a man. Initiators say that boys need a second birth, this time a birth from men.'[3] A father is in fact the key to this second birth. Unfortunately we have no special ritual in our culture today which would help this 'calling out' process. The writer and teacher Gordon Dalbey once taught in Nigeria, and describes graphically the initiation rite in rural areas. Apparently a boy lives with his mother until he is about eleven, and then one

---

[1] Samuel Osherson, *Finding Our Fathers* (New York: Ballantine Books, 1986), p. 6.
[2] ibid.
[3] Robert Bly, *Iron John* (Dorset: Element Books, 1990), p. 16.

evening the village elders and the boy's father appear outside the mother's hut. They start to call the boy out. The mother opens the door and shields her son from the men. But the men shout to the boy: 'Come out, son of our people, come out.' Standing behind his mother, the boy hesitates. Beside him and behind him is the safe and the known. 'Hesitatingly, wanting but not daring to look at his mother, the boy steps forth from the dark womb of his mother's hut into the outside – born again, this time as a child of the father.' Other boys in the same village are called out at the same time, and there follows a time of instruction into the men's world.

It is not necessary to subscribe to the details of these rituals. However, the fact that the need is recognised and a 'calling out' process is seen as integral to affirming manhood should be commended. Dalbey confesses that he weeps as he faces up to what he and his fellow twentieth-century Western males have lost:

> What does my own culture offer as a validation of manhood? The driver's licence at sixteen; and freedom at eighteen to join the Army, attend pornographic movies and to buy cigarettes and beer. The message is clear: becoming a man means operating a powerful machine, killing other men, masturbating, destroying your lungs and getting drunk.[1]

For his daughter, a father is the primary model of the opposite sex. He provides the initial interaction with the masculine gender. He is the first man to cuddle and kiss her, the first man she flirts with, the first man to prize her and love her. These experiences nurture the element which makes her different from him – her femininity.[2] When she reaches the threshold of womanhood, like the boy she awaits the masculine voice. Not to be called out

[1] Gordon Dalbey, *Healing the Masculine Soul* (London: Word, 1988), p. 50.
[2] H. Norman Wright, *Always Daddy's Girl* (Ventura, Calif.: Regal Books, 1989), p. 36.

from the feminine to the masculine, but to affirm her in the feminine. Earlier, father was needed to help her make the needed separation from mother; not too far away, but enough to know herself as an independent, fully autonomous person. Although by adolescence her sexual identity should be fixed, her femininity will not be in full bloom. It is still in bud, awaiting the masculine voice of affirmation. Few fathers realise how glorious and how necessary this task is.

If a father is unaware of his responsibility, or not available to perform it, a daughter will look elsewhere for the needed affirmation. Often she looks to other men and tries to gain their attention. If Dad has been available, then she is free of this need and can relate to the opposite sex in a natural and non-manipulative manner. We were recently having a meal with an American family, and the father told me the story of the ring his daughter was wearing. When she was sixteen she asked her father for a promise ring. He was surprised, because usually this is given to a girl by her first serious boyfriend. His daughter explained that she wanted to make a promise to him, as her father, that she would keep herself chaste until marriage, and as a sign of that promise she wanted him to give her a ring. When he told me that story I knew I was talking with a man who had done a good job in affirming his daughter's femininity.

Spiritual growth

Every child will have their first introduction to God through their parents. This introduction will come primarily through the father, not because he does all the teaching and praying, but by virtue of the fact that he is a father and will therefore reflect to the child the fatherhood of God. If this is a poor reflection or a marred one, then the child receives a wrong impression of God the Father which may be difficult to change later in life. But if it is a good one, then the child grows up with respect for God and trust in the goodness of God.

As we have already observed, Catherine Marshall was one of those fortunate people who had a wonderful relationship with her father. He was also an excellent introduction to God the Father. His lap was one of her favourite places, and for her his arms represented protection, reassurance, warmth, strength and nourishment. She remembered one Sunday morning sitting beside her mother in church, listening to her father preaching. At the end of the service he issued an invitation to those who wanted to accept Jesus as Lord:

> And suddenly I felt a stirring inside me. Very gentle. There was no voice or words, just a feeling of great warmth. I loved my father dearly. And I trusted him with all my heart. I loved him so much that I could feel tears forming behind my eyes.
>
> And then came the assurance. All along God had meant for the love of my earthly father to be a pattern of my heavenly Father and to show me the way to make connection with Him . . . It was the first encounter with the living God and my heavenly Father. The catechism had said that He had loved me first. So had my earthly father. He must have loved me even before birth while I was in my mother's body. Not only that, since I could love and trust my earthly father, how much more could I love and trust my Father in heaven – and then, without fear, place my future in His hands.[1]

A child watches his parents closely, and as he grows older he is making his own judgements on their behaviour. He knows how authentic and sincere is his father's Christian life and how real is his relationship with God. He recognises a life which is upright and true both at home and at church. These early experiences will be the foundations on which a personal faith is later built, or not built as the case may be.

Dr James Dobson was greatly influenced by his own

[1] Catherine Marshall, *Meeting God at Every Turn* (London: Hodder & Stoughton, 1981), pp. 30–1.

father. Even when he became a counsellor to millions he still leaned heavily on his advice. His father was away from home a great deal when James was young, so he would plan to spend as much time as he could with young Jim when he was at home. Some of the days spent hunting and fishing with his father were among the happiest of James' life:

> But most importantly, there was something dramatic that occurred between my dad and me out there in the forest. An intense love and affection was generated on those mornings that set the tone for a lifetime of fellowship. There was a closeness and a oneness that made me want to be like that man . . . that made me choose his values as my values, his dreams as my dreams, his God as my God.[1]

Practical fathering has many facets. Each one is important to the child's development. There is, however, one aspect of fathering which is not often spoken of. Perhaps it is largely ignored because it is a very Jewish concept, and a rather intangible one at that. It is expressed through the relationship between father and child and is very much tied in with a child's emotional and spiritual growth. The facet of practical fathering we shall now examine is a father's blessing.

[1] Rolf Zettersten, *Dr. Dobson: Turning Hearts Toward Home* (Dallas: Word, 1989), p. 28.

7

THE BLESSING

Dr James Dobson's father was the sort of man a son would want to emulate. The type of relationship they had enjoyed was the kind James endeavoured to establish with his own son, Ryan. When Ryan left home to go to college his father wrote him a letter expressing the feelings he had experienced on becoming a father: ' . . . a little lad named James Ryan made his grand entrance . . . He was my boy – the only son I would ever be privileged to raise. What a joy it was to watch him grow and develop and learn. How proud I was to be his father – to be trusted with the well-being of his soul.'[1] One can imagine how the boy would treasure such a letter: it would be read and re-read till every ounce of affirmation had been squeezed from it.

It is both a privilege and a responsibility to raise children and to have a part in shaping their lives. All the aspects of fathering already mentioned are of vital importance, and children whose fathers are able to meet the criteria are fortunate indeed. Often it is sheer lack of awareness which causes a father to neglect his responsibilities. This same ignorance prevents a man from passing on to his children the most valuable gift of all – his blessing.

Some people reading those words will immediately think to themselves: 'But I blessed my kids! They left home, went to college, got married – all with my blessing. I never stood in the way of what they wanted to do.' As

[1] Rolf Zettersten, *Dr. Dobson: Turning Hearts Toward Home* (Dallas: Word, 1989), p. 2.

valuable as this attitude may be, if we leave it there the fullness of the blessing will have been missed. What we are considering here is no haphazard, hit-and-miss activity, but a purposeful endeavour to pass on something of great value which you are persuaded is within your power, as a father, to grant to your children. And although a mother greatly enables a child to receive this gift, it is the father who is the main donor.

In the Jewish culture a father's blessing is of great importance. The roots of it go back many thousands of years to the beginning of time, when God blessed Adam and Eve and commissioned them to be fruitful, to fill the earth and subdue it (Gen. 1:28). The written account of Adam's line begins with his creation and blessing by God (Gen. 5:2). It was as if the act of creation was not enough. Once created, man needed a greater degree of involvement, a further touch from his Creator. He needed to be blessed with a future and he needed to be enabled and empowered to fulfil that destiny. This has been true for every person born since the first Adam.

God had a similar interaction with Noah after the flood. He blessed him and again told him to be fruitful and fill the earth (Gen. 9:1). Many years later God called Abram to leave his country and his father's household and said to him: 'I will make you into a great nation and I will bless you; I will make your name great, and you will be a blessing. I will bless those who bless you, and whoever curses you I will curse; and all peoples on earth will be blessed through you' (Gen. 12:2–3). At this point man became instrumental in passing on God's blessing to others.

Isaac is the first example of a father blessing his son. Old and nearly blind, Isaac decided the time had come to give his eldest son, Esau, his blessing. Rebekah overheard the conversation between father and son and conspired with Jacob to cheat Esau out of it. Rebekah prepared the food which Isaac loved and dressed Jacob in goatskin so that Isaac was tricked into believing he was blessing his hairy firstborn:

Then his father Isaac said to him, 'Come here, my son, and kiss me.'

So he went to him and kissed him. When Isaac caught the smell of his clothes, he blessed him and said, 'Ah, the smell of my son is like the smell of a field that the Lord has blessed. May God give you of heaven's dew and of earth's richness – an abundance of grain and new wine. May nations serve you and peoples bow down to you. Be lord over your brothers, and may the sons of your mother bow down to you. May those who curse you be cursed and those who bless you be blessed.' (Gen. 27:26–9)

There may have been deceit involved in obtaining this blessing, but there was no denying the reality of it. One of the most tragic cries in the Bible was uttered when Esau came home to receive his father's blessing and found it was too late: 'When Esau heard his father's words, he burst out with a loud and bitter cry and said to his father, "Bless me – me too, my father! . . . Do you have only one blessing, my father? Bless me too, my father!" Then Esau wept aloud' (Gen. 27:34, 38). Isaac does bless him, but it is not the blessing of the firstborn, which had already been given and could not be retracted. Clearly the blessing which Isaac passed on to his sons was linked with the future and their place in God's purposes.

Then Jacob himself grew old. Realising that his days were numbered, he blessed Joseph's sons Manasseh and Ephraim (Gen. 48:14). Then he gathered the rest of his family together and conferred on each one an individual blessing. Admittedly that took place long ago in a totally different culture, but there are certain basic components to Jacob's blessing which can give us direction as we consider how a twentieth-century father can bless his children.

The significance of the blessing

In the first instance our attention is drawn to the fact that Jacob had a different and appropriate blessing for each son (Gen. 49:28). To be able to bless so many children, each in a distinctive manner, surely indicates an intimate knowledge of each one and a big commitment of time spent listening to them, watching and praying about each of them. It would be impossible to come out with such relevant and fitting words without a high degree of natural knowledge about the child's character, his weaknesses and strengths, as well as that supernatural knowledge acquired only by waiting on God. From this we understand that a father's blessing indicates the value he places on each child and the commitment he has made to their present and future welfare.

Value
The words Jacob used to bless his sons were not those of a father who dashes in and out of the home and briefly acknowledges his son or daughter in passing. Nor were they words such as 'You look great son' or 'You're just gorgeous sweety', said from behind a newspaper, giving the child hardly a fleeting glance. Jacob proved that he valued his sons by the words he said to them. Only a father who knows his children intimately would be able to speak such specific and appropriate words to them. The words pointed to each son's future place in the purposes of God, and this too underlines a child's value not just to their earthly father but also to Almighty God. It speaks of a personal destiny which their father has recognised and acknowledged.

It is interesting to notice that the Hebrew verb 'to bless' is *barak*, which literally means 'to kneel'. This makes perfect sense when a person kneels before God to bless him, but is slightly more difficult to understand when the object of blessing is another human being; unless, of course, that person is in a position of authority and is worthy of honour. To kneel before someone is indicative of their value or worth to us. So for a father 'to kneel', figuratively speaking, before his children is to acknowledge how much they are valued by him.

Commitment

When a father is convinced that it is his responsibility and privilege to bless his children in a special way, then he will spend time waiting on God in order to get it right. He will desire to give a blessing appropriate to each child. He will spend time getting to know the character and abilities of each child. This all takes time and energy. Some fathers may already be committed to this, but to many modern-day fathers such a task may sound daunting. In a later chapter we will consider some ways and means of making this happen. For now, we should understand that what we are talking about is a whole-hearted commitment to the child's best interests. Commitment first takes a decision of the will and then a determined effort to complete the task.

The method of blessing children

Another aspect of Jacob's blessings which is helpful to notice is the manner in which they were passed on. We read that Jacob called for his sons: 'Gather round so that I can tell you . . . Assemble and listen, sons of Jacob; listen to your father Israel' (Gen. 49:1–2). The blessing which Jacob gave to each of his sons was special, but not secret. The content of each blessing may have grown quietly within Jacob over the years, but when the time was right it was spoken aloud to each of his children in turn. Joseph's two sons, Ephraim and Manasseh, were also blessed with words and also through the laying on of hands (Gen. 48:14).

Spoken words

Many fathers have positive thoughts about their offspring, but for different reasons never seem to get around to verbalising them. Perhaps embarrassment prevents them, or fear of generating pride, or they just never find the right opportunity. For whatever reason, most children receive more criticism than they do encouragement.

Words are powerful tools which can be used to curse or

bless, especially words said over a child about his future. Unthinking, negative predictions can mar a child for life. A disappointed father can so easily pronounce such words as 'You'll never make the grade, boy' to a son who has brought home yet another poor report. Instead of blessing, such a father curses his son. Negative words can have a lasting effect. This was brought home forcefully once as I prayed for a man who was plagued by perfectionism. He told me he was desperate because he was driving himself and his family crazy. As we prayed and I asked God to reveal to him what was going on, he began to cry. I asked him to tell me what was happening, and between sobs he said: 'I'll never please him, never.' Apparently his father had set very high standards which as a boy he had never been able to reach. As a result he had lived with a disappointed father who told him frequently that he would never amount to anything. Years later those words were still affecting him, and will continue to do so until he rejects the lies and tunes in to his heavenly Father's voice of encouragement and affirmation.

When I was at school I had to take sewing classes. A French lady taught us, and she became extremely irritated with my clumsy attempts at making a simple garment. Many times she told me despairingly that I was 'all thumbs' and would never learn to sew. Eventually I gave up, so convinced was I that I would never master a needle. When I got married my husband decided I must have an allergy to sewing because I was so reluctant to sew even a button on his shirt. Then a friend introduced me to tapestry, and even gave me a small one to practise on. With her encouragement I completed it and bought another. I went on to other sorts of needlework and found I wasn't 'all thumbs' after all. I could so easily have stayed under the curse of that negative prediction, and although I will probably never be a dedicated needlewoman, I am now free to enjoy the little I do.

If negative pronouncements have the power to impair a young life, conversely positive predictions have the power to encourage and spur children on to reach their full potential. They give a child direction and goals to aim for, and fill the mind with positive thoughts. In their excellent book *The Blessing*, Gary Smalley and John Trent state that children are filled with the potential to be all God intended them to be:

> It is as if the Lord places them on our doorstep one day, and we as parents are left as stewards of their abilities. During the years we have children in our home, the words we speak to them can wrap themselves around them like a cocoon. What we say shapes and develops their thoughts and thinking patterns. Loving words that picture a special future help children change and develop in a positive way.[1]

Every child needs to hear from his parents' lips that he is special, not only to them, but also special in God's sight. My parents were not very religious people, but by having all their babies baptised they indicated some belief in God. Certainly for me my baptism became an important event which helped to set the course of my life. My father and mother often referred to the day I was baptised as having been special. Apparently the vicar who took the service preached that evening, beginning his sermon with the words: 'Today I baptised a little girl called Mary.' For my parents those words set me apart, and because they seemed to believe it and told me often, I believed it too!

When our own children were growing up we knew so little of these matters. The good we did and said was often purely instinctive. But now we have more understanding and can be more purposeful with our grandchildren. We have tried to recognise and verbalise the specialness of each one, which for grandparents is not too hard!

Often it is merely a small incident which at the time impresses itself upon one's mind as something significant. It may be something the child does which indicates an embryonic gifting. It may be the child's name which

[1] Gary Smalley and John Trent, *The Blessing* (Milton Keynes: Word, 1989), p. 87.

holds special meaning, or the place he or she holds in the family. Whatever it has been in our experience, we have recounted it to the child to help him know that his life has importance.

In the past, names have held more meaning than they do today. They often described the circumstances of the birth, as in the case of Isaac. When the Lord told Abraham that Sarah would have a child, even though she was well past the age of childbearing, Sarah overheard and laughed. When his son was born, Abraham named him Isaac, which means 'to laugh'. Sarah said, 'God has brought me laughter, and everyone who hears about this will laugh with me' (Gen. 21:6).

Sometimes the name described the manner of birth but also contained a revelatory element. For example, Jacob was born grasping his brother Esau's heel, and so he was called 'he grasps'; figuratively this means 'he deceives'. This was an incredibly suitable name for Jacob, knowing how things worked out in his life. Isaac had named his son well, but did not have a full revelation. At a later date God changed his name. It took place at Peniel, where Jacob wrestled with the angel of the Lord all night and refused to let him go until he blessed him. So the angel said, 'Your name will no longer be Jacob, but Israel, because you have struggled with God and with men and have overcome'; and then 'he blessed him there' (Gen. 32:28–9). When God chooses a name, he chooses very appropriately. He instructed Joseph to give Jesus his name 'because he will save his people from their sins' (Matt. 1:21). It was a name which spoke of his future and of the significant part he would play in God's plan of salvation.

Our only granddaughter was born after several months of anxiety about her well-being. When she was eventually placed in her mother's arms, fit and well, Tasha exclaimed: 'By the Grace of God.' And so she was called Grace. Her name has special significance for us all, and I believe will prove to have been in some way prophetic.

Adopted children particularly need to have their specialness verbalised to them. The fact that they have been chosen can be stressed to show they are set apart and therefore unique. Choosing a name which holds some significance and contains within it hope for the future could also be helpful in emphasising a child's value.

Jacob chose a particular moment to gather his family around him in order to pronounce a blessing over each one. Most children would feel amply blessed if every now and again they could hear some positive comments from their fathers. However, far better if a father made a policy of verbally blessing each of his children as a general practice, and at particular times – such as birthdays, going to a new school, or a job – in some more specific manner.

Through touch

When Jacob blessed his grandsons Ephraim and Manasseh, he kissed them and laid his hands on their heads. In orthodox Jewish homes it is still the custom for the patriarch of the family to bless each member of the family with words and with the laying on of hands. In the Bible the giving of a blessing is normally associated with touch. When Jesus blessed the little children, he picked them up:

> People were bringing little children to Jesus to have him touch them, but the disciples rebuked them. When Jesus saw this, he was indignant. He said to them, 'Let the little children come to me, and do not hinder them . . .' And he took the children in his arms, put his hands on them and blessed them. (Mark 10:13–16)

Touch has the power to affect us physically, emotionally and spiritually. It can demonstrate affection or ownership. It can hurt or comfort. It can imprison or release a person. In the life of Jesus and the disciples it had the power to heal the sick. Throughout the history of the Church people have continued to experience healing through the laying on of hands. The apostles placed their hands on Saul and Barnabas for the work which God had called them to (Acts 13:3). Today the laying on of hands is still employed when commissioning people to special work. Timothy received a special gift through the laying on of the elders' hands (1

Tim. 4:14). And people are still receiving special anointing through the same means.

In family life touch is vital. However, the touch connected with the blessing we are exploring is more than the normal everyday touch which a child needs for physical and emotional health. It is a more purposeful touch, with the intent to bless in a special way. Nevertheless, a father who is naturally and consistently loving with his children opens the door and prepares them to receive the special touch of blessing when it is given.

When touch is used in conjunction with a father's spoken blessing it has special significance and will long be remembered by the one blessed. It demonstrates belief in the spiritual dimension of the blessing. It carries with it the authority of scripture and the weight of tradition. It also demonstrates a father's identification and oneness of purpose with his children.

As we have seen, Jacob's blessings were passed on verbally and through the laying on of hands. Although the actual content is not relevant to us, the two areas which Jacob highlights in his blessings would be appropriate in any culture, at any time.

The substance of the blessing

Although Jacob had words of rebuke for Reuben, he first underlined his qualities: 'You are my firstborn, my might, the first sign of my strength, excelling in honour, excelling in power' (Gen. 49:3). He then went on to predict Reuben's future, which Jacob saw would be the result of his tempestuous personality: 'Turbulent as the waters, you will no longer excel, for you went up onto your father's bed, onto my couch and defiled it' (Gen. 49:4). Unfortunately his lack of personal discipline had involved him in gross sin, which Jacob knew about and predicted would have dire consequences.

An acknowledgement of personal qualities

A committed father will have taken note of his offspring's positive attributes and will have been commenting on these throughout his life. When the time comes to give a more formal type of blessing, then these qualities should be highlighted. 'May God bless the gifts of leadership which you possess, and increase your intuitive understanding of others': these are the sort of words which could be pronounced over a son or daughter who has always taken the lead and seems to be naturally sensitive towards other people. At the same time, a father's responsibility is to see any dangers these characteristics could pose in the future, and if necessary to include a few words of warning. So the blessing could run as follows: 'May God bless the gifts of leadership which you possess. May he keep you humble, and may you learn to become a servant leader.'

Jacob's blessings did not just contain hope for the future they went a step further and included in each blessing was supernatural revelation about the destiny of each son.

Future predictions

When Jacob called for his sons in order to bless them, he said to them: 'Gather round so that I can tell you what will happen to you in days to come' (Gen. 49:1). What he then pronounced was partly prophecy from the Lord and partly predictions formed out of his intimate knowledge of his children's individual characters. If there is no thought of the future in a father's dealings with his children, then he will have failed in his responsibility. Certainly every father should be spending time thinking and praying about the way forward for his children. The conclusions he comes to, especially with regard to their future careers, will be drawn from his years of intimate involvement with them and should be expressed positively – never in a way that might cripple with a curse of negativity.

So often in these days parents allow the educational establishments to take over the job of launching their children into the future. They feel the schools are better equipped than they are to know their children's strengths and weaknesses, and sadly this is often true. Some of our school teachers have been splendid role models to make up for an absent father at home. But a father and a mother, not the school, should be in the ideal position to assess the child's abilities and, together with the child, to ensure as wide a base as possible upon which to build a future. This is in no way to undervalue the schools' opinions, which should always be highly respected. It is after all the parents, not the teachers, who have lived with the child day in and day out for fifteen years or so, and they should have an intimate knowledge of his future potential. Decisions should be made on the basis of this greater understanding. I remember our eldest daughter preparing for A-levels and thinking about her next step. A form mistress advised her to apply only to polytechnics for a place, explaining that the training was more practical and would suit her better. I was prepared to go along with whatever the school suggested, but David was not so sure. He knew Charlotte's character and abilities well and felt she should be given the chance to have a go for a different course at a certain university. The form mistress may not have been very pleased, but she could not override the parents. Time has shown the choice to have been the right one, and one which launched Charlotte into God's plan for her life.

As already observed, Jacob's predictions did not only come from his natural understanding, but also contained information which only God could have revealed to him. For example, the blessing for Judah is remarkable for its prophetic content: 'The sceptre will not depart from Judah, nor the ruler's staff from between his feet, until he comes to whom it belongs and the obedience of the nations is his' (Gen. 49:10). As we know, this was partly fulfilled in King David, who was from the tribe of Judah, but it came to full fruition in Jesus, who was born of the same tribe. Zebulun was told that his tribe would live near the sea, and 450 years later they settled within ten miles of the Mediterranean (Josh. 19:10). Gad was told he would be attacked by a band of raiders but that he would attack them at their heels. In fact, when he went back to Israel he lived east of Jordan and was very vulnerable to raids by the Moabites (Josh. 13:24). In this way Jacob blessed each son by revealing his future place in the purposes of God.

A committed father could most likely envisage himself blessing his children with words which come out of his knowledge of their individual gifts, as already mentioned. For example, a child may have consistently shown consideration and kindness towards others, and a father could draw attention to this in his blessing by saying: 'May God bless the spirit of love and mercy which I see in you. May God lead you into a future where you can use these gifts to his honour and glory.' This, I believe, would be a very appropriate and adequate way to bless one's children; by acknowledging the present and preparing them for the future. However, Jacob's blessing went a step further than that and actually contained a prophetic dimension which could only have been revealed supernaturally. I believe it is possible, and desirable, even in this day and age, to ask God for supernatural revelation concerning our children's future. Such insights may come through prayer, reading the Bible, dreams, visions, a prophecy from another person or member of the family. A few years ago David and I received a prophetic word from a friend about our family which was particularly pertinent at the time and therefore very reassuring.

When James Dobson accepted Christ there was great rejoicing in the family. First of all because it was a vital step in his spiritual pilgrimage, but also because it was the fulfilment of a prophecy given by his maternal great-grandfather, George McCluskey. 'This patriarch of the family was also a man of prayer who spent hours every day petitioning God specifically for the spiritual welfare of his offspring.'[1] During one of these prayer times George McCluskey felt that God had revealed to him that every member of his family for four successive generations would become a Christian. When a father

[1] Zettersten, *Dr. Dobson*, p. 27.

desires to have godly offspring he will, like McCluskey, spend time interceding on their behalf. But at the same time he could be asking God for revelation and insight with regard to their future.

Travelling recently in North America, I met a young man of about fifteen years of age. When I asked him what he intended to do when he left school, he replied that he would most likely become a pastor, like his father: 'You see, my Dad says that I have inherited his gifting.' I am sure his father was right. He may have made his prediction on the basis of natural knowledge of his son's abilities, but knowing the father I suspect he was also speaking out of a prophetic awareness of his son's future.

Dangers to be avoided

However, when a father blesses a child and makes reference to the future, there are some hidden dangers. One is the risk of steering a child towards a future which pleases only the parents. The other is placing a burden of expectation upon a child which he is too immature to carry.

Manipulation

A big temptation for a father is to plan a future for his child which fits his own dreams and aspirations. He rightly has a vision for his child, but it is one which does not take either the child or God into account. Such a plan lacks true awareness of his offspring's unique personality and particular gifts. It may be that he longs for a son who will follow in his footsteps, or for a daughter who will go to university and fulfil the dream he was prevented from achieving. He is blinded by such hopes, and sets out on a road which will only succeed in robbing his child of the blessing which would point him towards his own unique place in God's plan.

Expectations

Laying an unnecessary burden on a child is another danger
to be avoided. It is important to remember a child's
capacity to take in plans for the future. Not only is
each child different in the way he handles expectations
and suggestions, but also each child matures gradually in
his capacity to cope with expectation. A wise father will
intuitively know how much and when to share his vision
of the future with his children. One child may well enjoy
being told by his father that he has the makings of a doctor,
even though he is only ten years old. Another could feel
terrified at the prospect and may need to mature a little
before having such a possibility shared with him.

Bad timing

Another pitfall is sharing too soon significant dreams or
visions one has received about one's family. We are told
that Mary, the mother of Jesus, 'treasured all these things
in her heart' (Luke 2:51). It is not always right immediately
to share the things God may be showing you. It may never
be right. Sometimes a parent receives a word of prophecy
from another person or has a significant dream about a
child and is not sure of the interpretation. The best thing
in such circumstances is to wait and pray for the correct
interpretation and the right timing to share it with the child
concerned.

A father can avoid these dangers by making a commitment to know his children as thoroughly as possible. He
should take note of their particular gifts and spend time
waiting on God for further insight. Unselfish commitment
and prayer is necessary before he can bless each child with
a blessing which exactly fits him as an individual.

The time and place for blessing

It is easy to be haphazard in the job of parenting. The
rush and bustle of parenthood precludes us spending time
thinking out a policy. Yet unless we do think about certain
elements, they are likely not to be done, or to be done

inadequately. I recently prayed with a young boy of fourteen who was afraid he was developing homosexual tendencies. In fact he was at a very precarious stage of development and was in need of more specific encouragement from his father. His father was a caring man and more loving than many, but seems never to have planned any specific time to spend with his son. Consequently he had missed the tell-tale signs of anxiety.

In one sense the elements of blessing which we have underlined should form part of a child's everyday experience with his parents. As long as each aspect of the blessing is covered adequately, this may be sufficient. Many families would find it difficult or embarrassing to incorporate a formal time for conferring a special blessing on their children. On the other hand, putting a time of blessing into a more formal setting could be like the icing on the cake.

As a pastor, my husband blesses his flock continually. He may pass old Mrs Brown in the street and call out: 'How are you Mrs Brown? May God bless you.' Yet people often remark on the specialness of the blessing he pronounces at the end of a Sunday service. Both types of blessing are necessary, but one is given out of affection and the other out of responsibility and authority.

Practical fathering holds many challenges, not least the blessing of one's children. Settings for this more formal type of blessing will be suggested in a later chapter. Meanwhile, we will turn our attention to some of the possible effects of not being adequately fathered.

8

CONSEQUENCES OF FAILURE

Clearly many of today's fathers are struggling in their attempts to head up the family and to father their children properly. The society in which we live, the present economic climate, our own ignorance and selfishness are among the variety of reasons which inhibit us from being good parents to our children. Many of these factors are unlikely to alter dramatically. Only when parents themselves are convinced that the situation is critical will changes take place.

Clorinda was a young Mapuche Indian who had lived the first fifteen years of her life in a thatched 'ruca' somewhere in the foothills of the Andes. She had collected wood from the forest, helped her mother cook over an open fire, had never worn shoes and could barely read or write. She came to help me in the house when we lived in the Chilean frontier town of Chol Chol. It was no luxury to have help when every bucket of drinking water had to be drawn from a well and every loaf of bread cooked on a stove fuelled with logs cut up in your own backyard. For Clorinda, living with us was like being transported to another planet. The first time she saw our staircase she gasped with fright and began to climb it as if she were ascending Mount Everest. But Clorinda was a rapid learner. After a few weeks she found the quick way down the stairs via the banisters! Mostly she learned by trial and error – such as what you do with the multiple pips of the prickly pear. In a ruca you spit them out on the dirt floor. Our horror as we watched hundreds of pips strewn across our polished floors was enough to make Clorinda quickly realise her error. Trial and error are good teachers except when there is no second chance. I heard her cry out in fright one lunch-time; running into the kitchen, I found her clutching what had been a plastic bowl but was now a shrivelled mess. In her ignorance she had placed the bowl full of fried potato chips in the oven to keep warm.

Sadly, many men enter fatherhood in a similar state of ignorance. Their previous experience has not prepared them adequately for the care of immature, dependent creatures who are in the delicate process of development and for whom there will be no second chance to receive the care of a human father. Unfortunately, the previous generation of absent fathers, distant fathers and authoritarian fathers have left behind a mass of inadequately fathered people who, having themselves become parents, are now floundering with no one to guide them.

By and large society today is dominated by a mindset which distrusts natural instincts. When the hospital handed over our first baby to our care, we were nervous about taking responsibility for such a tiny, premature baby and looked for advice. I was firmly told not to feed her more than every four hours, not to pick her up between feeds and not to give her more than five minutes at each breast. I obeyed almost to the letter. I suppressed my gut feeling that wanted to feed her on demand and diligently followed the rules – but I could never find it in me to leave her to cry for long hours. I thank God today that I followed my maternal instincts in that matter. I wish I had in many other areas, but I believed my elders and betters!

Neither the medical authorities nor our elders, however, have always given good advice, and it would be wrong to trust the latest social trends just because they are fashionable. As we have seen, the health and happiness of our children have not been high on the list of priorities today. I would have been a better mother had I followed my gut reactions and not listened to others. In fact it has always been easier to be a good mother than a good father. A mother has the advantage of hormonal changes which prepare her for the job of motherhood. The hormones back up her natural instinct to stay near the baby. She enters a time of 'maternal preoccupation' which is not easily squashed, though society by and large attempts to do so. A father, on the other hand, does not have such advantages, and he can easily get swallowed up in the demands which his culture makes upon him, especially if there is no previous experience of good fathering to fall back on. It is interesting that in predicting the coming of the prophet, God says he will turn the hearts of the fathers to their children, and the hearts of the children to their fathers. God foresees the separation between fathers and their children as being in desperate need of mending. He says nothing about mothers and their children (Mal. 4:6).

The reason for highlighting the breakdown in the father-child relationship is not for the purpose of blaming fathers, but to draw attention to the pain and damage the failure is causing. It is always tempting to live in denial and avoid facing unpleasant facts. But when we face the truth, however difficult, we begin to long for changes and begin to pray and look for ways to right the wrongs.

So what is the truth? The truth is that the experience of an absent father, a distant father or a wounding father can wreak havoc in the lives of their offspring. This in turn rebounds negatively upon society, and everyone reaps the bitter fruit.

Bitter fruit in the lives of women

Promiscuity

'Research reveals that girls who enter into promiscuous sexual relationships at an early age almost always come from homes where fathers have been unaffectionate and have failed to meet the need of their young daughters to be touched and physically affirmed.'[1]

When Dad fails to offer his daughter appropriate intimacy she will inevitably look for it elsewhere; searching

[1] Gordon MacDonald, *The Effective Father* (Crowborough: Highland Books, 1989), p. 231.

hungrily for the love and affirmation which should have been hers by rights as a daughter:

> A study of 7,000 women who worked in strip joints or topless bars revealed that most of the women came from absent-father homes. The researcher commented that most of these women conceded that they were probably looking for the male attention that they had never gotten during their childhood.[1]

Sandra came for counselling because she felt so empty inside. She looked more like a teenager than the mother of four children. Her voice was rather childish, and her way of dressing would have been more appropriate for an adolescent. Before she had become a Christian she had filled an aching inner void in many different ways. In the privacy of the counselling room the sad story of those years of searching for love poured out. Before marriage she had been promiscuous, and after marriage had been unfaithful on several occasions. She felt degraded and ashamed. As we talked she revealed that her father had always been very distant and during her teens he had seemed particularly embarrassed by her. As she sobbed out the memories of those unhappy years she confessed that when she realised that affirmation was not coming from her father she had looked for it from other men. But her promiscuity had not made her feel any better about herself. Not only did she continue to have an empty void inside, she also felt increasingly unacceptable. Even though her husband would try hard to affirm her, she always remained in doubt about herself. It was as if a part of Sandra was still waiting and listening for that paternal voice of affirmation. The way through for Sandra, after she had confessed and repented, was to properly grieve the loss of her father, not through death but through ignorance and negligence. Furthermore, she had to accept the fact that he was not there for her emotionally, and never would

---

[1] Josh McDowell and Dr Norm Wakefield, *The Dad Difference* (San Bernardino: Here's Life Publishers, 1989), p. 61.

be. Only from the reality of that emptiness was God able to meet her need and fill the gap in her life.

Frigidity and shame

Unlike Sandra, Margaret and Adele had fathers who were loving and available to them, but sadly they both overstepped the proper boundaries of behaviour with their daughters. Adele's father became very attentive when she reached puberty and would insist she sat on his lap while he stroked her and placed his penis between her legs. Margaret's father never actually touched her, but would let his eyes run over her body in a way which made her feel very uncomfortable and ashamed. Both women were damaged as a result of this relationship. Adele was unable to respond sexually to her husband. From her teens she had suppressed her femaleness and dressed in boyish clothes which disguised the shapely body beneath. Margaret, on the other hand, was feminine and attractive. She dressed perfectly in an attempt to cover her feelings of shame and self-rejection; feelings caused by her father's excessive attention at a particularly self-conscious age.

Appropriate affection and affirmation from a father assure a girl that she is acceptable. They allow her blossoming femininity to develop normally and open the door for healthy sexual relationships in the future. However, when the normal affection between a father and daughter crosses the line and turns into inappropriate intimacy, she is left with a host of painful and conflicting feelings with regard to herself and men in general.

The 'eternal girl' or the 'armoured Amazon'

Regardless of a child's home environment, whether it be rich or poor, the sort of relationship a girl has with her father affects her for the rest of her life: 'You can't see a bad daughter-father relationship written on a woman's face. Instead the fruits of the absence of a healthy relationship are borne on the heart.'[1] The writer and analyst

[1] ibid.

Linda Leonard exposes in *The Wounded Woman* the deep trauma suffered in the emotions of women who fail to receive the care and guidance they need from their fathers. In her female clients she has found two opposing patterns which frequently result from a wounded relationship to the father. One pattern she calls the 'eternal girl'; the other, the 'armoured Amazon'. The 'eternal girl' is the woman who has remained psychologically a child even though she may be sixty or seventy years of age. She remains for always a dependent child. She looks and acts the innocent, helpless, passive victim. She fails to control or direct her own life.[1]

The 'eternal girl' fitted Marilyn exactly. Her wide, baby-blue eyes would look at us innocently as she explained what a helpless victim she was. Her father had been a difficult, authoritarian man who ruled his family with a particularly stinging form of sarcasm. With this weapon he was able to shame Marilyn and shrink her self-esteem to nothing. As her father he had had the power to bless or curse her. He chose to curse with his cutting sarcasm. Consequently her psychological development was for ever impaired. She remained the 'eternal girl'.

In contrast, the 'armoured Amazon' occurs as a reaction against inadequate fathering:

> In reacting against the negligent father such women often identify on the ego level with the masculine or fathering functions themselves. Since their fathers didn't give them what they needed, they find they have to do it themselves . . . But this masculine identity is often a protective shell, an armour against their own softness, weakness, and vulnerability.[2]

Sadly, the tough, masculine woman is only too common in our present society. Watching people file into a recent conference, my attention was drawn to a grey-suited priest.

---

[1] Linda Schierse Leonard, *The Wounded Woman* (London: Shambhala, 1982), p. 15.
[2] ibid., p. 17.

At first glance he appeared to be a man, but when I took a second look I wasn't too sure. My dilemma was resolved the next day when the same priest appeared wearing a grey skirt in place of the trousers. Maybe she felt the need to enter what had previously been a man's domain by looking like one, or possibly she was protecting her feelings of vulnerability with masculine dress. Could the 'armoured Amazon' be just a cover-up for the 'eternal girl' – that vulnerable, weak, unprotected, needy child who dwells within the heart of every woman who was not fortunate enough to have a father who protected, supported, cherished and affirmed her?

In many instances a girl's father will not be absent or abusive. He will be an ordinary father who works hard and cares for his family. If such a father is able to make himself available emotionally and physically to his daughter when he is at home; if he is able to affirm her and encourage her and pass on the message that she is of great importance to him, he will be doing a good job of fathering. However, some men fail to do this for the simple reason that they do not know how, or because they do not realise what an important part they play in their daughter's life. As a result she may be left unaffirmed in her femininity, unsure of herself as a woman, and lacking the confidence to do as well as she could do socially and professionally.

Bitter fruit in the lives of men

As we have already suggested in an earlier chapter, the two world wars, the Great Depression and the rise of militant feminism are much to blame for the lack of involvement fathers have today in family life. Whatever the reasons, this withdrawal has been far-reaching in its effects on individuals and on the community.

Homosexuality

The homosexual issue is a hot potato. People hold differing views. One common explanation current today to account for some men's preference for their own sex is a prenatal

brain hormonalisation which influences their subsequent
sexual status or orientation. If this is the case, nothing can
be done to change or reorientate such people. However,
Dr Charles Williams, a psychologist and family therapist,
feels the evidence is inconclusive. He says that this view

> represents the current popular trend of assigning responsi-
> bility for the way we are to genes, heredity, physiology,
> or hormones. This view places little responsibility upon
> the individual, family, environment, or outside influ-
> ences which have a significant effect on one's identity. It
> also ignores the concept of 'free choice'. The physiologi-
> cal approach predestines one to a sexual orientation,
> and it leaves no chance to alter that destiny.[1]

Dr Williams goes on to say that one of the earliest
interpersonal psychological theories was that the homosexual male was the result of a dominant mother and an absent
father. The mother's dominance was seen as the primary
cause, and the father's abuse or absence a secondary one.
However, one area which has received very little in-depth
examination is the father-son relationship. Williams goes
on to review

> what may be the greatest outside factor in determining
> a son's sexual orientation – his father's influence. Boys
> need men to help them learn how to identify with and
> become comfortable with their masculinity. The depth
> and quality of a father-son relationship affects a boy
> more than most ever realize.[2]

Apparently Dr Tim LeHaye once claimed that he had
never counselled a homosexual who had had a good
relationship with his father. Joseph Nicolosi, a psychologist working with homosexuals, supports the view that
homosexual feelings in men are a psychological condition
resulting from 'incomplete masculine identification'. He
also notes that all his clients had poor relationships with

[1] D. Charles Williams, *Forever a Father* (Wheaton, Ill.: Victor
Books, 1991), p. 144.
[2] ibid., p. 147.

their fathers. Richard Green, a professor of psychiatry and the author of books on homosexuality, agrees that 'fathers are the most important influence on their sons' development into men'. He recommends that 'fathers stay close to their sons and model the virtues they want them to emulate'. Dr Elizabeth Moberly, a research psychologist and lecturer, maintains that 'most men who engage in homosexual behaviour do so because of the deficit in their relationship with their fathers'.[1]

An over-identification with the feminine

Whatever we believe about the causes of homosexuality, a father's presence is crucial to a boy's sexual development. This has been detailed in a previous chapter, but it is so vital as to be worth underlining once again. A boy, like a girl, starts his life connected in the most intimate and dependent way to his mother. He spends nine months attached to her through the umbilical cord, and then for the next few months is probably attached to her breast for several hours a day. At first he cannot distinguish himself from her. They are one. Even when he becomes aware of being a separate individual he remains emotionally close to his mother. She represents comfort, softness and security. Though he may still be very attached to her, by the time he is three, and progressively thereafter, he should be separating his sexual identity from his mother and be identifying with his father. It is hard for a little boy to make this separation without an attractive, available male figure to call him away from the soft, warm femaleness of his mother. When that figure is not available, several things may happen. The boy may remain over-identified with the feminine and fail to cross over to the masculine. This could mean he becomes a 'soft male' who enjoys the more intuitive, creative activities which belong predominantly to the female. At the same time he may lack the masculine attributes of power to initiate and the courage to make decisions and take the lead.

[1] ibid., pp. 152–3.

We need to remember in all this that a mother on her own finds it very difficult to initiate separation, which is why the father is so important. Left to her own devices, her instinct is to hold on to her son and provide him with all the nurture and support which it is in her power to give him. As far as she is concerned he will be her little boy always and she his mother. A popular American short story which is enjoyed by both children and adults is called 'Love You Forever'. It illustrates the enduring nature of a mother's love for her son. The book follows a baby through the various stages of childhood until he reaches manhood. All through the years the mother is depicted as creeping nightly into her son's bedroom and softly singing a song to him:

> I'll love you for ever,
> I'll like you always,
> As long as I'm living
> my baby you'll be.[1]

We may feel deeply moved by such loving sentiments, but without a good father around to prevent his son remaining fused to his mother, this could have disastrous results for the boy.

Ricky came into the category of a boy dominated by his mother and lacking the attractive father-figure to interrupt the closeness. Ricky perceived his father as weak and unappealing and had no desire to be near him, nor had his mother encouraged him to leave her side. She had been a dominant controlling force all his life and he desperately wanted to be free from her influence. He was a gifted man, creative in many ways, but often lacked courage to say 'no' when it would have been appropriate to do so. He found it hard to initiate and to take decisive action. He was gentle and feared strong women. In fact if one tried to get too close he would break out in a sweat and feel physically sick. None of this changed until Ricky began to

[1] Robert Munsch, *Love You Forever* (Ontario: Firefly Books, 1986).

experience God as his Father, be blessed and affirmed by him, and finally be called away by God from his mother into his true masculinity.

Rejection of the feminine

Another route for a young boy without a father to aid him in the separation process is rebellion. Because he instinctively knows his manhood is in danger, he may break away from his mother's control in defiant anger. Unfortunately, in rejecting her he also rejects the feminine aspects of himself. He then continues on through life as the 'macho' man, lacking softness, intuitive understanding and creativity, which are the more feminine attributes which would balance his personality and contribute a richness to his masculinity.

Delinquency

As we have seen, the absence of a father-son relationship often has serious spin-offs. The boy suffers during childhood, his adult relationships are frequently marred, and, besides these personal consequences, society also suffers. In his bestselling book *Iron John*, Robert Bly writes of the importance of moving from the mother's realm to the father's realm. He says that 'never being welcomed into the male world by older men is a wound in the chest'. He then goes on to relate some remarks the police chief of Detroit had made about the young men he arrests, who not only do not have any responsible older man in the house, but in fact have never even met one. He said that when you look at a gang, you are looking at young men who have no older men around them at all. 'Gang members try desperately to learn courage, family loyalty, and discipline from each other. It works for a few, but for most it doesn't.'[1]

The rise in violence and crime is put down to many factors – e.g., poverty, unemployment, poor housing – but seldom to the breakdown in family life. Dennis and

[1] Robert Bly, *Iron John* (Dorset: Element Books, 1990), p. 32.

Erdos, in their study on crime in the inner cities, point out that today we have more state benefits and better housing, and yet there is a huge rise in crime. They show that at other times in our history when there has been high unemployment there has not been the same rise in the crime rate. Conversely, in the mid-1970s, when unemployment was at a low ebb, the crime rate rose inexorably. In fact, 'the period of the steepest rises in crime has been a period of unprecedented, and quite possibly historically unrepeatable prosperity'.[1]

The studies of Dennis and Erdos show that unless a child is brought up in the constant atmosphere of human beings who are negotiating the business of getting on with one another, co-operating, controlling their anger, effecting reconciliations, he cannot learn what it is to be an effective member of a social group.[2]

Research also indicates that delinquency, particularly in boys, is an area where the father's rather than the mother's role is important. Delinquency is usually accompanied by a poor father-child relationship. When a father is absent there is no accessible role model. It is from the father figure that a boy learns such things as delay of gratification, and how to control aggressive and destructive impulses.[3]

The breakdown of relationship between a son and his father is very costly in terms of the individual personal suffering. It is even more disturbing in terms of the corporate suffering in society. We hear daily reports of violence on the streets. Old people are being mugged in their own beds for nothing. These facts alone should force society to look seriously for the true reasons behind the problem.

---

[1] Norman Dennis and George Erdos, *Families Without Fatherhood* (London: IEA Health and Welfare Unit, 1992), pp. 96, 99.
[2] ibid., p. 74.
[3] Patricia Morgan, in Richard Whitfield (ed.), *Families Matter* (Basingstoke: Marshall Pickering, 1987), p. 44.

Rebellion

Absent or negligent fathering may be the most likely cause for delinquency and rebellion, but an additional reason for this sort of anti-social behaviour can be found in a different type of fathering. Authoritarian, rigid fathers may go on frustrating and provoking a child until in seething anger he punishes the demanding parent by deliberately doing the opposite of what he knows would be their wish. St Paul exhorts fathers not to exasperate their children (Eph. 6:4). A gentle, quiet child may be easily cowed into submission by an over-bearing parent, but a strong-willed child will struggle not to be annihilated by a domineering father and will exert his personality through rebellion.

Bitter fruit for everyone

Men and women carry different wounds as a result of a damaging relationship with their fathers. But often the consequences are common to both. For example, the self-esteem and self-confidence of either sex can be badly damaged as a result of poor fathering.

Feelings of worthlessness

The absence of a father may leave a deep need for approval and may cause such a child to look for it long past childhood.

Len was a capable young man who had worked hard and gained a significant position in the business world. Despite his obvious success he was privately full of self-doubt. Because these nagging worries about his own value affected his working relationships, he sought some help. In the presence of his counsellor, Len asked God to show him the roots of his problem. He immediately remembered that his father had walked out on his mother and himself when he was four years old, and had never come back. With this memory, feelings of insecurity and worthlessness began to surface, accompanied by some incorrect and immature interpretations he had put on the event. He believed that somehow he had failed to win his father's approval and that his father had not valued him enough to stay with him. This sense of worthlessness had been buried within his heart all that time and had never been resolved. It exerted adverse pressure upon him whenever he was put in a position of needing support and approval from a male authority figure.

Perfectionism

Drawing on his personal counselling experience, Gordon MacDonald suggests that when a father doesn't speak the language of affirmation, or when it is not marked with affirmation but rather with ridicule, sarcasm and disgust, then disaster follows.[1] Any type of shaming deals a mortal wound to a child's self-esteem from which the child may never recover.

Lucilla's father had not deserted her, in fact he was very much present throughout the whole of her childhood. Her predominant memory of her father was of a demanding man whom she was never able to please. He wanted her to be successful and was disappointed at any sign of failure. Her exhausting need to get everything just right was the legacy of this unaffirming relationship.

Poor social and educational performance

In their research Dennis and Erdos cite the 'Crellin' study made of 17,000 children at the National Children's Bureau. Of these children, 600 were born outside of marriage. The children of 'un-committed' fathers and 'committed' fathers were spread evenly throughout the social classes. The children of 'un-committed' fathers were shown to have below-average grades. On the Southgate reading test, nearly half of the children of the 'un-committed' fathers fell into the bottom grade of 'poor'; they were five months behind in 'arithmetic age', and they were also shown to contain a higher proportion of maladjusted children.

As previously noted, factual surveys like Crellin's show

---

[1] MacDonald, *The Effective Father*, p. 24.

that on average the lifelong socially-certified monogamous family on the pre-1960s pattern was better for children than any one of a variety of alternatives.[1] The fact is that without the encouragement of both a father and a mother children are likely to suffer educationally and socially.

Depression

The result of negligent fathering may also cause self-doubt and periods of depression. It is interesting to read the biography of the late Conservative prime minister Sir Harold Macmillan. His father Maurice was somewhat of a workaholic and spent long hours at the office. Possibly he was escaping from a domineering wife. Some regarded her as something of a 'fiend'; so tough and powerful that she inhibited all three sons, making them repressed and withdrawn. As a child Harold hardly saw his retiring father. With his extremely demanding mother and taciturn, withdrawn father, his childhood must have been far from happy. During childhood he developed a proneness to despondency, known as the 'Black Dog': '"I was oppressed by some kind of mysterious power which would be sure to get me in the end . . ." The Black Dog was to ambush him from dark corners for the rest of his days . . .'[2]

Harold Macmillan's depression was of a cyclical kind, and he usually retreated behind a book until it had passed. I once had cause to pray for a lady who suffered from a chronic form of depression. Her mood was always grey, and had been for as long as she could remember. Her childhood had not been particularly traumatic, but had lacked any real show of affection. One of her earliest memories was of her father playing with her little brother, who was the delight of his life. She would watch, feel sad, and then go to her room and look at a book. Was it

[1] Dennis and Erdos, *Families Without Fatherhood*, pp. 32, 40, 42.
[2] Alistair Horne, *Macmillan, 1894–1956* (London: Macmillan, 1988), pp. 10–13.

any wonder that an air of sadness pervaded that lady's whole life?

The truth is that children are damaged and later suffer painful consequences whenever they have not had the opportunity to form a good, satisfying relationship with their fathers. The questions we must now ask ourselves are: Can the damaged be repaired? Is there healing for the fatherless? And can men who have never been affirmed by their fathers recover their true masculinity?

9

HEALING THE EFFECTS
OF FATHER LOSS

Eleanor Roosevelt lost her father just before her tenth
birthday. She said of him: 'He dominated my life as long as
he lived, and was the love of my life for many years after he
died.'[1] In her book *Father Loss*, Elyce Wakerman points
out that when a girl loses her father she is 'deprived of the
first man she ever loved, and she will carry that rejection
with her for the rest of her life'.[2] John, another of the 'Lost
Boys' on the recent television programme, recorded the
death of his father in his diary with the few short words:
'The worst day of my life. Dad died.'[3]

Many books have been written about the healing of
emotional damage. I have myself added to their number.
It is not my wish, therefore, to write in detail about a
subject so thoroughly covered. But for the purposes of
this book I will list briefly the steps which are of particular
importance when it comes to the process of being healed
from the devastating loss of a father's love.

Acknowledgement

The first of these is acknowledgement. Some children are
so embarrassed, even shamed, by the loss of a parent
through death or divorce that they refuse to talk about it.

[1] Elyce Wakerman, *Father Loss* (London: Piatkus, 1986), p.
271.
[2] ibid., p. 55.
[3] *Everyman*, 'Lost Boys', BBC1, 29 November 1992.

They may admit the actual loss, but what they frequently deny is the pain and confusion which that loss has caused them, because the loss embarrasses them. Repression is so much a part of our culture that we are often unaware of how easily we do it and how effectively we bury our pain. By a shrug of the shoulders and a refusal to face it, the child pretends it does not matter. Children may convince themselves they really are not affected and that it was better for Dad to have gone away – 'After all, he was nothing but a problem when around the home, and I was glad when he went.' Often there really is a sense of relief when an abusive father is at last off the scene, but what is forgotten is that a bad father, like a good, dead father, is the same as 'no father', and not having a father leaves a child bereft, not only of a father, but to some degree of a mother also. She is often so overwhelmed with grief or rejection, and so exhausted by the effort to keep things going, that she is unable to be emotionally present for her child.

A child needs the love and attention of an accessible male and female during the vulnerable years of childhood. When these two people are not easily available, there is a sense of loss which may have a lasting effect upon the child. Acknowledgement is the first step to healing this injury.

In my experience, women are usually more in touch with their feelings than men. When pressed, they will admit to the reality of their loss. A man usually begins by saying that he does not think the loss of his father affected him much. When the tragedy happened he just got on with life. Sometimes it helps a man to acknowledge the pain of his loss if he is encouraged to talk about it and describe the feelings he had at the time. Women, on the other hand, will remember the pain they experienced. They may even admit to moments of pain in the present. For example, when they catch sight of a young girl and her father relating affectionately together, they may feel a momentary pang of jealousy or self-pity.

Mourning

Once the truth of one's condition has been recognised, the next step towards healing is to allow oneself the experience of grief. A loss of a parent, for whatever reason, has to be mourned before the negative consequences can be laid to rest. Few children are given the opportunity to grieve at the time of loss. Children today are better prepared for the facts of life than the facts of death. Elyce Wakerman writes:

> There is little question that repression is one of the major components of father loss. Of the fatherless women in our study, only 18 percent were encouraged to express their feelings at the time of loss. And even now, as adults, 30 percent say that they have not as yet accepted it. As long as feelings are repressed, the woman maintains a fantasised attachment to her father that precludes attachment to others, for just as acknowledgment is a prerequisite to mourning, so mourning is a prerequisite to separation.[1]

One reason for repression when the loss is through death is that the remaining parent is often too caught up in his or her own grief to appreciate the loss to the child. Equally, with divorce a mother or father is so devastated by rejection and hurt that he or she may not realise the painful interpretation the child could be putting on the event. Nor may the parent understand how necessary it is for the child to talk over thoughts and feelings. Other adults present are frequently ignorant of the child's need to express the confusion and pain in order to come to an early acceptance of loss. Therefore the help the child needs is not forthcoming.

John, who lost his father as a young boy, was excluded from the adult grief immediately after his father's death. During those hours he came to the conclusion that he was going to have to be brave. Consequently he never properly

[1] Wakerman, *Father Loss*, p. 236.

grieved his loss. Years later, attending a counselling course, he was being supervised while he counselled another person and the session touched on the counsellee's relationship with his father. John suddenly found he had gone blank, and he looked to his supervisor for help. His supervisor perceptively asked him about his own father. Then came a great explosion, as a wave of grief swept over John and he burst into uncontrollable sobs.[1]

One of the reasons a child represses his grief is the fear of being overwhelmed by an unbearable pain which he instinctively feels ill-equipped to handle. This is probably the case unless a strong, caring adult comes alongside the child, giving him permission and making it safe enough to express his feelings fully. However, once childhood is left behind, unless a person's ego strength is greatly depleted, it should be possible in the safety of a therapeutic environment to reconnect with the buried pain of loss and to express it. The therapeutic setting may be a counsellor's office, but equally it could be a group which has met for the purpose of emotional and spiritual growth. In many instances people connect with suppressed pain for the first time at a Christian conference. I recently attended a conference directed solely towards the pursuit of sexual wholeness. Many of the delegates had come from abusive or cold backgrounds. It was with a sense of relief that they were able, for the first time, to cry openly about the loss and the pain they had endured.

Grief which has been suppressed for many years often rises and explodes out of a person like a volcanic eruption. It comes from deep within and may erupt with great cries of anguish. When this happens, the resolution is likely to come quickly. On the other hand, the grief could surface more slowly and may then last for weeks, even months.

Laurie was a young girl from a cold, unaffirming home. She believed she had been actively disliked by her mother and ignored by her father. When she eventually began to experience the pain of her dismal childhood, she entered

[1] *Everyman*, 'Lost Boys', BBC1, 29 November 1992.

a period of great sadness. During the counselling sessions she wept copious tears; during the week she silently mourned her loss. Only slowly did she begin to glimpse the light at the end of the tunnel.

The loss of a father through preoccupation, busyness or negligence differs, of course, from loss through death or divorce. There is no definite moment of severance on which to pin the grief. Instead, a child is in a continual state of deprivation but does not know exactly what is missing. Nevertheless, that natural but unrequited longing for paternal love eventually adds up to a loss as real as one caused by death. So it is that in most cases the loss of a father will not have been fully recognised or mourned at the time.

For an adult trying to come to terms with the loss of a father, the next step after acknowledgement should be grief. No one enjoys pain, and even when we are mature enough to handle it most of us will automatically take avoidance action the moment we feel its onset. In fact the step of grieving can easily be aborted, and this may happen in several ways.

Mistaking intellectual insight for resolution

A moment of understanding can be very powerful. Many years ago, during a counselling seminar, I was asked to write a description of both my parents. I knew and understood the effect my mother's rather unpredictable personality had had upon me. But what I had never given much thought to was my father. He had always been a rather shadowy, distant figure. As I sat, pen poised, I realised for the first time that the lack of relationship with my father had affected me as deeply as had my relationship with my mother. I silently digested my new-found knowledge, and for the time being it was sufficient. I would have left it there, except for the fact that resolution and change did not accompany the revelation. It needed more than that. It needed appropriate expression.

Unproductive anger

Anger is another abortive route. When the full extent of the childhood wounds is eventually acknowledged, anger at the loss will inevitably follow. Anger is a normal stage in any bereavement, but when indulged in for too long it may spiral into self-pity. When this happens to someone, they seem unable to come to terms with what has happened. It is as if, in their minds, acceptance equals agreement with the abuse, negligence or desertion, and forgiveness equals forgetting that it ever occurred. Neither of which is true. Acceptance means agreeing that our fathers have fallen short of God's standards, as we all have. Absent fathers are more than likely themselves the products of equally absent fathers. This makes them as much victims as ourselves. Forgiveness takes place when we give up our desire to punish, and instead hand our fathers over to God, who alone knows the whole truth.

The American TV hostess Oprah Winfrey recently interviewed several people who had been badly hurt by a close relative or friend. On the show, she attempted to reconcile them to one another. One woman of about thirty years of age was extremely angry with her mother for deserting her when she was a child. Her parents had divorced, and she had remained with her father while her mother had married again and gone abroad with her new husband, and had not been around for any of her daughter's important achievements. The daughter was seething with resentment towards her mother and said she would never forgive her. As I watched the show I felt very sorry for her, but was struck by the ugliness and unproductiveness of her bitterness. It was not going to give her back any of the things she had lost. It was poisoning her present, and it was certainly not going to give her a happier future. In fact she was robbing herself and her family of the first step towards reconciliation with the mother she had longed for.

Anger is always a secondary emotion, which means that beneath it is a primary feeling that needs healing. It is also a defensive emotion. It protects a person from feeling the pain of loss, and when retained it prevents any final healing from occurring. Nevertheless, anger is a step in the process of bereavement, and few manage to reach any resolution without at some time passing through this phase.

Some find it difficult to move on from this stage, and the reason may be that the anger is verbally acknowledged but never emotionally released. When anger is deeply felt and appropriately expressed with energy, the heart is quickly rid of the bitterness and a person can move on. Inappropriate expression would be to the wrong people at the wrong time and in the wrong places. The appropriate setting would be the privacy of a counselling room, with a counsellor or with a mature Christian friend.

Manipulating others
Another way to abort healing is to recognise the injury, begin to experience the pain of it, and then attempt to ease the pain by seeking a surrogate parent. The hunger for love, encouragement and affirmation may be so great that a person feels driven to alleviate his gnawing emotional hunger by some means. It never works! No human being can be the parent we long for, nor would it be right for them to try. The end result of such an unhealthy alliance would be disappointment and eventual disillusionment. Honest-to-goodness grief may be painful and difficult, but it is the only route which leads to resolution.

Acceptance

When the grief work is done, acceptance can be embraced. The resolution so long sought is in sight. As has already been said, acceptance is not agreement with sin. It is an acceptance which says: 'That's how it was. My Dad hurt me by what he did (or didn't do), and sinned against me, but we are all fallen creatures and he was as much a victim as I was.'

Forgiveness

Acceptance eventually produces the fruit of forgiveness, which is a soothing balm to the sore wound of loss. As forgiveness flows, grace abounds and a deep healing comes to bind up the broken-hearted.

Resolution

At this point those whose fathers are still alive may find themselves desiring a reconciliation and hoping for some emotional closeness before it is too late. In some cases this may be achieved, but for many there will be no such happy ending. However, resolution is still a possibility, even though one's emotional needs may never be met by one's earthly father. God wants to show that he is sufficient to meet all our needs. He has gone to great pains to demonstrate his love for us. As we have already established, God is a perfect Father, and when a person comes into a living relationship with him a gradual transformation takes place. Through the word of God, the conviction of the Holy Spirit and the love of the Christian family, a sense of self-worth and security are slowly restored. An earthly father may never have been prepared to take time off from work or give up a morning's golf for a child. He may have begotten a child and then walked away from the responsibility of fathering, leaving the child bereft of security and any sense of real worth. But God the Father so loved us that he sent his own beloved Son to die in our place. What more proof do we need of the value which God places on each one of us?

A new inheritance

Not only is personal worth restored, but we also become participators in an inheritance of value far greater than we would have received from any earthly parent.

I was reminded of this when praying for Daniel. He was sitting hunched, head in hands, looking every bit the deprived child he had once been. Although he was now a man of nearly forty, the years of abuse and rejection by his father were still producing bitter fruits in his life. His work, his marriage and his family were all suffering as a result. As I began to pray, the words of Jesus came to me: 'Blessed are the poor in spirit, for theirs is the kingdom of heaven' (Matt. 5:3). If I had ever seen a man who was poor in spirit, I saw it in Daniel then. He was emotionally poverty-stricken. He had received so little in the way of encouragement, affirmation or affection that his cup was empty and he seemed to have nothing to give to his wife and children. But Jesus had said that such people were blessed because theirs is the kingdom of heaven. I could feel hope welling up in my heart for Daniel. The negligence of his earthly father had left him 'poor in spirit'. Now, that very impoverishment made him eligible to be an heir of his heavenly Father's blessings. In the present Daniel was still experiencing the poverty of his childhood, and although it could be some weeks before he would enter fully into his new inheritance, the promise was there.

Many people like Daniel have been deprived of the priceless inheritance of an earthly father's presence and blessing. But God has promised to be a Father to the fatherless (Ps. 68:5). Jesus taught his disciples to call God their Father. When they prayed, they were to address God as 'Our Father . . .' (Matt. 6:9). When his soul was overwhelmed with sorrow to the point of death, Jesus called out to his Father (Matt. 26:38–9), and in that moment of great need he chose the familiar, child-like term of 'Abba, Father' with which to address God. The Holy Spirit encourages a similar familiarity from those who have come into a position of sonship: ' . . . but you received the Spirit of sonship. And by him we cry, "*Abba*, Father." The Spirit himself testifies with our spirit that we are God's children. Now if we are children, then we are heirs – heirs of God and co-heirs with Christ . . .' (Rom. 8:15–17).

All earthly relationships pale in comparison to those in God's kingdom. We are called to be children, bearing the family likeness, with intimate and unlimited access to our Father. As co-heirs with Christ, we are participators of the riches of God's kingdom – now in part, but later in full: 'In my Father's house are many rooms . . . I am going there to prepare a place for you' (John 14:2).

10

RECOVERING TRUE MASCULINITY

Two particular emotional traumas are suffered by those who have never enjoyed a satisfying relationship with their human fathers. One is the 'hole in the heart' syndrome – the emotional void. This may leave a gnawing pain, often difficult to identify, which may be retained even into old age unless healing can be found along the way. Many substitutes or gap-fillers may be tried, but only a father can actually relieve that ache and fill the void. Once the years of childhood are past, then God alone can be such a father.

The other commonly inflicted injury affects the masculine soul in particular. The paternal rift can damage a man's masculinity, causing him to limp his way into marriage and fatherhood without ever having been initiated into an authentic masculinity or ever having received a role model on which he was able to base his gender identity. He may look for authentication from other men, from women, from work, or from the differing models presented by the media. But these are false trails which leave a man unsatisfied and unfulfilled. The search for true manhood is still gathering momentum.

Influenced by Robert Bly's bestseller *Iron John*,[1] American men have been trekking into the woods for 'wild man' weekends in their efforts to discover that lost manhood. Bly's book is about a boy becoming a man. Through an interpretation of the Grimm brothers' mythological story of Iron John, Bly takes the reader on an imaginative

[1] Robert Bly, *Iron John* (Dorset: Element Books, 1990).

journey through a type of male initiation into manhood. Iron John is the wild man of the forest who causes anyone who enters the woods to disappear. The king's huntsman eventually captures him, and he is held prisoner in the palace courtyard. The key to his cage is given to the queen, who places it under her pillow. One day the young prince is playing in the courtyard and his golden ball rolls into the wild man's cage. To retrieve it he has to steal the key from under his mother's pillow and set Iron John free. Fearing his royal parents' response, the prince then runs off into the forest with Iron John. Through the experience of poverty and hardship the boy becomes a man and enters the service of a nearby king. He longs to become a warrior, and Iron John helps him by supplying his mount. The young man rides to battle and is victorious for the king, who rewards him with the hand of his daughter in marriage. Through the prince's bravery Iron John becomes free of his enchantment and recovers his true identity, that of a powerful, baronial king.

Bly's book, though a mish-mash of myths and New Age philosophies, contains many insights and corresponds closely with other writers on the same subject. He correctly identifies some of the problem areas for boys growing up in today's society. He graphically highlights important steps in the discovery of authentic manhood. For example, the key to freedom is in the queen's keeping. The boy has to steal it before the journey to manhood can even begin. Then, through the experience of wounding, loneliness, poverty and servitude the boy becomes a man. Finally he emerges as the conquering warrior – a picture of true manhood.

Gordon Dalbey is a Christian minister and lecturer. In his book *Healing the Masculine Soul* he also tackles the subject of man's damaged masculinity. It was while attending an anti-pornography film that he began to question why men would seek such evil. 'What brokenness do we bear that has led us to seek saving power in pornography, instead of in You?' he asks God. 'Where have we lost the deep and abiding sense of our healthy masculine sexuality that we would turn to so sick a substitute?' However, a war has many battles, a campaign many fronts, and while fighting pornography he suggests that we should not ignore the primary front itself, namely the wound in the masculine soul. 'Certainly,' he writes:

> men do not fantasize before Playboy centrefolds because we are so courageous before real-live, three-dimensional women, but rather, because we fear them; we do not beat up women because we are so strong, but rather, because we feel so powerless before them; we do not impregnate women and leave them to consider an abortion because we are so self-reliant, but rather, because we feel inadequate to be responsible fathers and husbands.

With our image of true manhood so distorted and damaged, he says, 'our task as men today is not to curse our manhood but to redeem it, in the true prophetic sense'.

Dalbey identifies the 'wound' with great sensitivity, and using biblical images leads the reader not to the woods, but to the cross for healing: 'For the Good News that we men long for today comes only in the terrifying, painful initiation of the Cross in which we die to our proud natural self and rise anew as sons of the Father-God.'[1] He also identifies the steps a boy must take in his journey towards true manhood. He demonstrates the need for a 'calling out' and some ritual of initiation which would enable boys to leave the security of their mother and take their place alongside the men. Like Bly, he sees authentic masculinity portrayed by a warrior.

Bly and Dalbey have approached the initiation and discovery of manhood from different standpoints, although many of their insights are similar. Of course they both share one thing in common. Both are men, and are therefore in a better position to identify the problem. Obviously for me, being a woman, it is not so easy.

[1] Gordon Dalbey, *Healing the Masculine Soul* (London: Word, 1988), p. 21.

However, women have been, and still are, affected by the problem, and when men are healed and take up their rightful place in the family women will experience a deep measure of healing also. Bearing all this in mind, I propose to examine the question of true masculinity by asking three questions. In the first instance: What is the root of man's woundedness? Secondly: What is true masculinity? Lastly: How can true masculinity be restored?

What is the root of man's woundedness?

In the beginning, the world God made was good. Adam and Eve enjoyed the security of oneness with God, within themselves and with each other. The work they were given gave meaning to their lives and a sense of significance. Their identity would not have been an issue until they succumbed and partook of the forbidden fruit. In that moment of disobedience to God, separation, division and enmity became a first-time reality. Adam and Eve experienced a separation from God, a schism within themselves, and a flawed relationship with each other.

Immediately following the fall, they became self-conscious, as if they had looked into a mirror for the first time and seen themselves. In *Perelandra*, C. S. Lewis depicts the tempter as offering Eve, the Green Lady, a mirror in which she can see herself. He tells her: 'That is what it means to be a man or a woman – to walk alongside oneself as if one were a second person and to delight in one's own beauty. Mirrors were made to teach us this art.'[1] So instead of being God-conscious, man became self-conscious.

Their next reaction was one of fear. They hid from the Lord because they were afraid to be seen naked. Up to that point in time they had enjoyed an unhindered relationship with their Creator. Now they experienced the primal pain of separation. This happened first of all with God, but

[1] C. S. Lewis, *Perelandra* (London: Pan Books, 1943), p. 125.

then inevitably, as they began blame-shifting, with each other also.

Ever since then men and women have carried a woundedness within themselves. They have become divided beings on many different levels. However, one of the marks of this woundedness was the loss of authentic masculinity.

Between the time of the first Adam and the coming of Jesus, the second Adam, many men crossed the stage of human history. All manifested their woundedness at different times and in different ways. One of them, Moses, started life with no father to guide him and as a young man depended upon his physical strength and privileged position in life to achieve his ambitions. Only after forty years in the desert did he become the man God wanted him to be.

Jacob was another who as a boy was alienated from his father. This was partly through his father's favouritism of Esau, but also because of his mother's controlling influence. He demonstrated a patent lack of manliness when, still dominated by his mother, he cheated Esau out of his blessing. He did not begin the journey towards true masculinity until after he had left home and had begun to fend for himself. He finally became the man God intended when he wrestled with God and his name was changed to Israel.

Joseph was also separated from his father at a young age, partly through his own fault. He angered his older brothers by his insensitive boasting and flaunting his 'specialness' before them. Only after years of suffering and hardship did he reach his true stature.

All these men, at times during their lives, depended for their masculine identity upon their position in life, personal attributes or other people. Like the young prince in the story of Iron John, they only found their true masculinity after years of hardship and suffering.

What is true masculinity?

From the beginning Adam lived in relationship with God and was wholly and perfectly man. He had no need to search for any identity apart from God. After the fall his relationship to God was broken and he was no longer a whole person. His search for identity in other ways began. At one point man even tried to make a name by building a city, with a tower up to heaven (Gen. 11:4).

Appearance, occupation, position, possessions, success, strength, family and sex are some of the most familiar methods of identification. For example, a man of seventy, though happily married, was discovered in a compromising position with a young woman. All his adult life he had defined his masculinity in terms of his sexual prowess. Now, fearing its decline, he felt driven to testing out his masculine powers. Another man of fifty spends hours of his time in some energetic sport. His life revolves around keeping fit and looking good. Masculinity depends upon it!

Yet even these methods can change. In the 1960s and 1970s the gentle, understanding male image was 'in', but in the 1980s it was the tough image. For all the searching, no satisfactory model of manhood has yet been universally acclaimed. Let us remind ourselves that the first Adam lost it. Could this mean that the second Adam regained it?

'For God was pleased to have all his fulness dwell in him, and through him to reconcile to himself all things, whether things on earth or things in heaven, by making peace through his blood, shed on the cross' (Col. 1:19–20). Jesus is the great reconciler. He is able to reconcile man to God. He also reconciles man to man, and by his grace he can heal the trauma within the heart of man. Being fully human, he is also an example for all humanity, both male and female. In his character and his attitudes he became a model for us all. He said: 'I am the way and the truth and the life' (John 14:6). He also provides us with the power to become like him (2 Cor. 3:18). However, Jesus was incarnate as a full-blooded male, and as such is a model of perfect manhood for men. In our search for a true understanding of masculinity there are aspects of Jesus' life which are particularly relevant.

Separation from his mother
Jewish boys were accepted into a man's world when they reached the age of twelve. For Jesus, this was most likely celebrated when he went up to the Temple for the Feast of the Passover with his parents, since Luke specifically states that he was twelve years old (Luke 2:42). From that time he demonstrated an awareness of emotional separateness from his parents and began defining himself by his relationship to his heavenly Father. When his parents left Jerusalem, Jesus stayed behind in the Temple, evidently without their knowledge. When they eventually discovered him, his mother rebuked him. But Jesus had taken his initiation into manhood seriously and presumed his parents had done the same. He gently explained his behaviour to her: 'Didn't you know I had to be in my Father's house?' (Luke 2:49).

The modern mind often finds his reply bewildering. How can Jesus be a model for us and seem to speak to his mother in such a disrespectful manner? Unless one understands the issue of emotional separation from mother and initiation into manhood, it may seem incomprehensible.

Today's Western society does not provide any acceptable model for making a separation which is recognised by all parties. Instead, the recognition of manhood is an issue which is either not handled at all, or is at best handled clumsily and inadequately. In the next chapter I have indicated some possible ways of righting this omission.

A young boy entering his teens, with or without a ritual, has to take some specific steps away from boyhood and towards manhood. For a start, he needs to put some emotional distance between himself and his mother. Up until this point he has probably enjoyed quite a degree of intimacy with her; sharing his life with her. Now he needs to be moving away from his mother towards greater intimacy with his father. A good father will be making opportunity for more man-to-man talks. A young teenager will also want to spend more time with his friends. He will begin to admire and copy older males; his youth leader, prefect or master at school. For a few years his attention will be focused on more manly occupations. Later his interests will include females, but it will be from the different perspective of a man to a woman instead of a boy to his mother.

Unless this separation from mother is negotiated in some way at the right time, when it does come later it is frequently painful. This was brought home to me recently when listening to the comedian Bob Monkhouse being interviewed by Dr Anthony Clare on his *In the Psychiatrist's Chair* programme on Radio 4. Bob was discussing his relationship with his parents. His mother had been the dominant person in his childhood. He had felt close to her, though not to his father, whom he perceived as being a weak man. Dr Clare suggested that there may have been an 'Oedipal' problem between him and his mother, in other words too close a relationship between mother and son which excluded father. This surprised Bob, until they explored the relationship in more depth. His mother had had a poor relationship with her husband, but had obviously favoured Bob. For him she had been the only woman in his life throughout his childhood and adolescence. However, when he went into the forces he met a girl whom he decided to marry. His mother refused to attend the wedding, and for twenty years would not speak to him – just because he had got married! Oedipal problem or not, it would appear that there had never been an appropriate emotional separation between mother and son at the right time. When it eventually came, much later, it was very traumatic.[1]

The incident in the Temple during the early life of Jesus highlights this important milestone. If it was a necessary step for Jesus in his journey to manhood, perhaps twentieth-century adolescents also need some similar ritual. This is emphasised by both Bly and Dalbey. Bly devotes his first chapter to 'The Pillow and the Key'. In order to liberate the wild man, the young prince had to steal the key from under his mother's pillow – signifying

[1] *In the Psychiatrist's Chair*, BBC Radio 4, 31 December 1992.

the power a mother has over her son's masculinity, which has to be taken from her if manhood is to be achieved. Dalbey dedicates several chapters to the necessity of a boy being 'called out' from his mother and received into the male domain as an entry into manhood.

Years later in the life of Jesus, Mary tried once again to pressurise him. The incident took place at a wedding feast in Cana of Galilee. Mary told Jesus about the wine crisis, although he was only a guest. '"Dear woman, why do you involve me?" Jesus replied, "My time has not yet come"' (John 2:4). By resisting his mother he was signalling firmly that his time was no longer under her control. He was fully committed to his heavenly Father's will.

Wielding the sword of truth
Jesus was tempted in all ways like us. The attack Satan launched against Jesus in the wilderness epitomises the 'dirty tricks campaign' which he launches against all God's children (Matt. 4:1–11). This desert experience also preceded three years of peak ministry in the life of Jesus.

Twice Satan challenged Jesus' identity: 'If you are the Son of God . . .' (vv. 3, 6). Then, having sought to sow seeds of doubt, he suggested ways for proving his identity: 'Tell these stones to become bread' (v. 3). In other words: 'Use your power to satisfy your personal needs and prove to everyone that you are the Son of God.' Then he suggested Jesus test his Father's love for him by throwing himself off the highest pinnacle of the Temple to see if God would send his angels to save him (vv. 5–6). Each time Jesus responded to Satan's challenge with the words: 'It is written . . .' (vv. 4, 6, 7). He wielded the sword of truth – the word of God. Satan then played his trump card. He offered Jesus a short cut to success and fame – the world's method of gaining identity. He took him up to a high mountain and showed him all the kingdoms of the world and their splendour: '"All this I will give you," he said, "if you will bow down and worship me"'

(v. 9). The very thing Jesus had come to do was being offered him on a plate. All he had to do was worship Satan. Jesus, like a true warrior, immediately wielded his sword again: 'Away from me, Satan! For it is written: "Worship the Lord your God, and serve him only"' (v. 10). At this Satan gave up. He could not withstand a champion who firmly raised the bright, shining sword of God's word.

As we have sought to demonstrate, Jesus' identity was firmly rooted in his relationship with his heavenly Father. He did not need to prove it either by his own power or by trying to manipulate God. Nor could he be tempted at the idea of getting to the top the easy way. His goal in life was to do the will of his Father and to serve him only. True masculinity belongs to men who survive the hardships of the desert and become warriors; men who recognise the enemy's strategies and defeat him by wielding the sword of truth.

Leadership and authority

Natural leaders have disciples who follow without coercion, manipulation or bribery. Jesus was such a man. 'Come,' he said, and grown men left their families and jobs to follow him. Jesus never demanded respect, but he received it nevertheless; not just from his intimate friends, but from those who heard him teach: 'the crowds were amazed at his teaching, because he taught as one who had authority, and not as their teachers of the law' (Matt. 7:28–9). He did not boast of a degree from a prestigious university or sit at the feet of a famous rabbi. He did not come from a rich family or possess any special physical attributes. He had none of the normal means for gaining the respect of others. But his remarkable personal stature and dignity were esteemed by all who knew him.

Looking after a family is a job for two, and both parents have equally responsible roles within the family. However, as already mentioned, a study carried out in the United States has shown that the healthiest families were found to be father-led.[1] A good father brings security into the family because of his natural leadership abilities. He does not need to exert his authority in any excessive manner, any more than Jesus had to. A man who is truly masculine has a bearing and a stature that commands respect and love without having to spell it out.

Self-discipline and courage

The two qualities of self-discipline and courage go together. It takes courage to be self-disciplined when people all around are bent on pleasing themselves. Jesus straddled two worlds when he was on earth. He belonged in heaven but lived on earth. He was fully human and fully divine. Somehow he managed to survive with people tugging him in all directions. He stood out in contrast to the religious and cultural leaders of his day. Their values were worldly and selfish, and Jesus was not afraid to confront their hypocrisy. Even for his friends he would not sacrifice his integrity. Peter, who had given up everything to follow him, received a sharp rebuke when he countered Jesus' announcement about his death. Mary and Martha, who had frequently given Jesus hospitality, were kept waiting when their brother was sick, because God's timing was more important than pleasing his friends.

During three pressurised years in the public eye Jesus maintained his equilibrium through the intimacy he enjoyed with his heavenly Father. At the beginning of those three years he spent forty days in the desert fasting, a period which terminated with a ferocious attack by the enemy which he courageously resisted. During his years of ministry the demand of the crowd drained his resources continually, and yet he often rose early in the morning to pray. Without time spent in his Father's presence he would not have had the energy or the courage to continue. Being human, only self-discipline enabled him to maintain that relationship with the Father.

[1] Robin Skynner, *Explorations with Families* (London: Methuen, 1987), p. 295.

Like Jesus, Christians straddle two worlds, and it is not easy to keep a balance between them. It is a difficult position, to be in the world and yet not of it. Besides these two worlds, there are other worlds people are forced to straddle, such as those of work and the family. Only courageous and self-disciplined men can keep those two worlds in their correct perspective and simultaneously maintain their poise.

No fear of feelings

One of the great myths of our day is that real men do not show their feelings. The stiff upper lip has been associated with bravery since Victorian days. Only women, as the weaker sex, are allowed to be emotional.

Yet Jesus showed a variety of feelings. He cried with the sisters at the news of Lazarus' death. He wept over Jerusalem. He was incensed by the improper use of his Father's house by the money-changers. Frequently he was moved with compassion by the suffering around him. When the mothers brought the children to him, he had time for them. He gently took them in his arms and blessed them. As a whole man, he manifested a full range of feelings. Men who seek to suppress their emotions in order to appear more manly are being duped by a false assumption. The Perfect Man, Jesus, was not afraid to show his feelings, either privately to his friends, or publicly before a crowd.

Writing on *Men and Masculinity*, Roy McCloughry feels that this is important

> because there are many men who believe that men were not made to display those characteristics which our society considers feminine. They talk of 'the feminised male' with derision, believing that men are meant to display aggression, ambition, autonomy and control, but not tenderness, vulnerability or other emotions. If Jesus is a norm for men then he must give us hope that being a man is a sufficient basis for displaying everything that is associated with being human . . . If it were not

possible for men to weep, be gentle or nurturing then the portrayal of Jesus as doing these things would be a cruel taunt.[1]

Dependence upon God

Religion has been called the opium of the masses – an anaesthetic for the poor; something that lulls the uneducated multitude into a false sense of happiness. God was no comforting drug to Jesus, someone just to fall back on when things were tough or when he was in trouble. His relationship with God was more important than life itself. He daily lived doing his Father's will: 'My food is to do the will of him who sent me and to finish his work' (John 4:34). His dependence never faltered.

Spirituality is popular today, but too many people seek a spiritual experience on their own terms. It has to be at their convenience and under their own control, which makes Christianity the least popular option. Christianity is all about giving up one's life to God and allowing him to direct one's paths. It is a life of dependence, which is the reverse of what most men view as masculinity. According to the world's way of thinking, a strong man is independent – a master of his own destiny, making people and situations work for him. If that means manipulating or controlling others, so be it. That's the cost of being a man in a man's world!

If Jesus were incarnate in today's world, there might be some things he would do differently, but his dependence on God would be exactly the same. He depended on God to the extent that he subordinated his own will to that of his Father's. 'Not my will but yours be done,' he said as he wrestled before God in the garden of Gethsemane, sweat like drops of blood falling to the ground.

He may have looked weak and beaten as he hung on the cross, but it was no wimpish weakling who, despite excruciating pain, could give comfort to a dying thief;

[1] Roy McCloughry, *Men and Masculinity* (London: Hodder & Stoughton, 1992), p. 141.

who found the moral strength to ask God to forgive those who were perpetrating this crime against him; who made arrangements for his mother's care when he was gone. No, this was a true man and a perfect model for men everywhere.

Even for twentieth-century man, Jesus is still an example of perfect manhood. McCloughry says that he finds himself asking, 'What would Jesus do in this situation? How would he respond to this person?' For him, Jesus is the ultimate hero: 'If I want to know about God I ask, "What is Jesus like?" If I want to grow as a human being I ask, "How can I be more like Jesus?"'[1]

How can true masculinity be restored?

Any man who would be whole should meditate on the life of Jesus until that divine model of manhood grips his heart as no other. This is a necessary step in the recovery of true masculinity, but this alone will not heal the wounds in the human heart.

Let the sword do its work

David was a warrior king, and he had the courage to ask God to point the sword of truth in his direction: 'Search me, O God, and know my heart; test me and know my anxious thoughts. See if there is any offensive way in me, and lead me in the way everlasting' (Ps. 139:23–4). The first step towards authentic manhood is to pray that the sword of truth be directed towards the heart:

> For the word of God is living and active. Sharper than any double-edged sword, it penetrates even to dividing soul and spirit, joints and marrow; it judges the thoughts and attitudes of the heart. Nothing in all creation is hidden from God's sight. Everything is uncovered and laid bare before the eyes of him to whom we must give account. (Heb. 4:12–13)

If a man desires true manhood, then at some point he

[1] McCloughry, *Men and Masculinity*, p. 134.

must take his stand before Almighty God and ask to be shown what is in his heart – the motives for what he does, the ambitions and goals which drive him; what sort of husband, father, friend he is; how like Jesus he is.

When the sword has flashed and revealed the truth, the next step is to ask God to wield it against your proud flesh; against any false dependencies you may have discovered – your position, your power, your appearance, your sex. Against any self-centredness. Against the things that entrap you and cause you to sin. Let him separate you from the feminine; from any identification with the opposite sex which may be blocking the development of true manhood. Perhaps you are trapped by the anger and rebellion with which you attempted to free yourself from the feminine.

Let the sword circumcise your heart, stripping away the calloused flesh until it is rendered sensitive and vulnerable, giving you a heart that will courageously respond to God's voice, to the truth and to others.

On several occasions I have witnessed the Holy Spirit bringing a man to the place of truth about himself. One time it was a young man who had become emotionally involved with another man, and although nothing sexual had taken place it was an unhealthy alliance. He excused his behaviour for some time, until one day God showed him the truth. He broke down and wept tears of repentance. The hardness of heart which had kept him in denial about his sin was cut away and his heart was made soft and pliable. Another time it was a young, handsome, enthusiastic man who had dreams of becoming an evangelist. One day the Holy Spirit convicted him of sexual sin with his girlfriend. As the sword did its work, he thought his heart would break. He will never be the same again. A far humbler man has emerged.

Ask God the Father to call you out

It is impossible to hear the voice of God calling you forth until the sword has done its work. Only then are you free to leave the clamouring voices of your mother, father, work, ambition, self; anything which may have tied you into a false image of masculinity. The sword's work is painful; but once it is done, then a man is free to connect with 'the deeper masculine Source which calls a man out – even from his father – to fulfil his unique, individual calling. The Christian man may trust that such a transcendent manhood is rooted in the Father God who created all men and beckons him through Jesus.'[1]

In the process of being 'called out' by God, a man may pass through a period of hardship and suffering. This is often God's way of refining and preparing a man to become a warrior who can be trusted and reliable in battle. Only after Jacob had spent twenty years serving Laban did he have the amazing experience of wrestling with God and receiving the new name of Israel. Joseph went through several years of imprisonment before he was freed and elevated to a position of leadership. It was after Moses had spent forty years in the desert tending his father-in-law's sheep that from the burning bush God called him to become a leader of his people. Jesus was taken into the desert for forty days and went through a time of severe testing before he entered upon his ministry. No man should be surprised if he is taken through a period of rigorous training before he can become a trusted warrior in the service of the King of Kings.

Take up the sword

To enter battle without a sword would be folly. If the enemy is to be routed, then prowess as a swordsman is vital. Joshua, the man who succeeded Moses and led the people into the promised land, was told:

> 'Be strong and very courageous. Be careful to obey all the law my servant Moses gave you; do not turn from it to the right or to the left, that you may be successful wherever you go. Do not let this Book of the Law depart from your mouth; meditate on it day and night, so that you may be careful to do everything written in it.' (Josh. 1:7–8)

[1] Dalbey, *Healing the Masculine Soul*, p. 54.

If the land is to be conquered, then the sword must be wielded daily by brave men. In the first place, men must become acquainted with the truth as it is in the word of God. Only by meditating day and night will it take root in a person's life. Then it must be used courageously. Firstly by allowing it to shape one's life, and then in the defence and extension of God's kingdom.

King David was a great warrior. Anointed at a young age, he became a popular hero. But a time came when he grew tired of wielding the sword in defence of his kingdom. He let others go to war, and he stayed at home. Without his sword in his hand and without the enforced discipline of battle, David grew slack and fell into sin with Bathsheba. When he discovered she was pregnant, he took a coward's way out and compounded his sin by arranging for her husband to be killed in battle so that he could marry her and hide his shame.

For a warrior, there is no respite; no moment when he can lay the sword down. It must continue to shape him and defend him. It is also an offensive weapon which must be used against the temptations of the enemy and against the structures and false values of the society in which he lives. It is time the warriors joined the battle behind the King. It has been said that for evil to flourish it is only necessary for good men to do nothing. Society will not change until brave men stand up for that which is good and true. That is not to say it will be easy: 'For our struggle is not against flesh and blood, but against the rulers, against the authorities, against the powers of this dark world and against the spiritual forces of evil in the heavenly realms' (Eph. 6:12).

God, the Eternal Father, can heal the wound in the hearts of fatherless men. He can call them forth into true manhood and bless their masculinity. In Jesus, men have a perfect role model. He wielded the sword of truth deftly and fearlessly. He calls Christian men to follow him, for he is 'the way and the truth and the life' (John 14:6).

11

SUGGESTIONS FOR BUSY FATHERS

It is reassuring to know that God in his mercy can bind up the broken-hearted and be a Father to the fatherless. Nevertheless, we long to see changes in our society which would result in more children, not less, growing up and enjoying their father's love and protection. It is only as individuals sort out their priorities and make changes in their lives that society will be affected. So, finally, we must seek some solutions to the problems which face fathers today.

Once a man comprehends how vital his presence is to the lives of his children, he will look with favour upon any advice which could enhance his relationship with them. However, every father's circumstances are different, and these suggestions will not necessarily be helpful to all. However, they may serve to encourage more creative thinking on how to optimise the fleeting years your children are with you.

Spending time with your children

'Most children equate love with time.'[1] If you value a relationship with your children, then somehow you have to make it a priority in your life and plan to spend time with them.

a) Make an arrangement each week to be with your children doing something they would like to do. The

[1] Josh McDowell and Dr Norm Wakefield, *The Dad Difference* (San Bernardino: Here's Life Publishers, 1989), p. 77.

appointment has to be as immutable as one made to see your doctor or dentist. Occasionally a polite but firm 'no' may have to be said to a boss in order to keep such a commitment.

b) Make a decision to listen attentively to what your children may have to say to you. Ask questions about what they think and feel. 'Most of us do not realize that emotions or feelings are conveniently limited to only four major categories of *mad, sad, glad* or *scared*. Each of these, of course, consists of varying degrees, levels of intensity, and differing ways we describe our emotions.'[1] So when a child tells you about something that happened at school, a response such as 'That must have made you feel mad/sad' would indicate understanding and encourage more sharing.

c) Try seeing life through their eyes. The best father is the one who is able to recapture his own boyhood.

d) Never fail to apologise to your children when you are wrong. Remember you are a model to your child, not just of manhood, but of Christian discipleship also.

e) If at all possible, take your children one at a time to your place of work and show them what you do. This gives mother a break, each child some individual time, and allows them to share your world for a short while.

Recently a friend of mine told me that her husband had taken their four-year-old daughter to the office with him. He had planned the day with his secretary, and together they had looked after her. Consequently the mother had had a free day, the secretary had had a change, which she enjoyed, and the little girl had had some special time with Daddy.

f) Try taking one of your children with you every time you have to run an errand.

g) When you are forced to be away from home for any length of time, make sure your children know how much you regret not being with them. You could phone them

[1] D. Charles Williams, *Forever a Father* (Wheaton, Ill.: Victor Books, 1991), p. 65.

every evening at their bedtime and have a short chat with each of them. Even when you are occasionally obliged to stay late at the office, a phone call at bedtime would demonstrate your love and interest.

h) Tell your children frequently how much you love and appreciate them.

i) Take the time to look at the work your children bring home from school and give them plenty of positive encouragement.

j) Make a special effort to attend parents' evenings at school, and be sure you are fully aware of your child's progress.

Communicating your faith

Not only are your children likely to project their impressions of you as a father on to God, but their relationship to God will be influenced by yours.

a) Share your faith with them in ways they can understand, and explain why you do certain things. But try to avoid sermonising!

Early one morning, before leaving for work, a friend of mine was praying and waiting on God when his small son interrupted him. 'What are you doing, Daddy?' he asked. 'I'm talking to God and waiting for him to give me a prophecy for the day,' answered the father. The following weekend, when the father was leading family prayers, the little boy asked his father to pray over him and give him a prophecy from God. It was a special moment as the father responded to his son's request.

b) Have your children's needs in mind when you choose a church. Make sure it has a good children's ministry and that it is a church which is relevant to young people. It is worth even changing one's denomination for the time that one's children are small, to ensure they are catered for.

c) If you are not able to have a family prayer time every day, try setting aside a special time at the weekend. Friday evening or Saturday morning could become family time, when everyone is able to share their week and their prayer needs for the week to come, pray for one another and read the Bible together. Perhaps Dad could make a habit of coming home earlier on a Friday evening and buying a Chinese takeaway, or something else popular with everyone, as a treat.

Plan fun time together

When our children look back over their childhood, the fun times are what they remember best. Camping holidays, picnics in the country or on the beach, tobogganing in the snow. Those are the times that stand out in the memory of a child.

a) Take a good book to read aloud to your children on holiday. My husband started this when our family were quite small, and the last time we did it was when they were in their late teens and we were on one of the last family holidays before they became independent.

b) Join up with cousins or another family and play rounders or wide games in the local park.

c) Try taking your children to the local pool for a swim at the weekend. If the pool is near enough, early Sunday morning, before church, could be a possibility. With the children out of the way, Mother could do other things more easily, and everyone could still be ready for church on time.

d) Turn the garage into a games room where you can set up a snooker board and table tennis. Or set up a netball basket in the backyard. Then make a point of playing with the children whenever you can.

e) Plan to learn a new sport alongside your children, such as windsurfing, sailing, skating, tennis or golf.

f) Try planning a fun evening together. Give Mum an evening off, and you cook the supper with the help of the children. After supper you could take out a family video and all watch it together.

Initiation into manhood for sons

It is important that you spend time with your sons from
childhood. They need to have their sexual identity separate
from their mother's by the time they are three years old.
A child will not find this easy unless Daddy is readily
accessible. Once your son has reached the age of thirteen
he is ready for an initiation and welcome into manhood.
Only a father (father figure) or grandfather can do this.

a) Have a special 'Bar Mitzvah' or 'Welcome to Manhood' dinner party and invite other male members of the
family, as well as your son's friends.

b) Give him presents which mark his new manhood. For
example, an electric shaver or a new study Bible. Perhaps
you could open a savings account for him and give him a
lesson on keeping a personal account book.

c) Celebrate by taking your son for a weekend away,
just the two of you. Go camping, windsurfing, canoeing
or climbing together. Spend some time talking about
manhood and the new experiences and responsibilities
which lie ahead for him.

Affirming your daughter's womanhood

At twelve or thirteen your daughters will start their
periods, and to all intents and purposes become women
able to have children of their own. As with the boys,
there is still a lot of growing and maturing left to do,
but physiologically they are women. It is important for
them to accept the changes which are happening to their
bodies and to be affirmed in their femininity. Mother
has a great part to play in her daughter's life, but the
affirmation of her femininity will come through her father.
Many grown women are still listening for that voice of
masculine affirmation. They feel unsure of themselves,
are ashamed of their sexuality, are unhappy with their
bodies. Sadly, many will wait in vain. It is not that these
women are not fully feminine, but that their womanhood
has not been blessed and therefore has not blossomed in
all its glory.

a) Without embarrassing her or drawing too much attention to her, when your daughter starts her periods tell her how proud you are of her.

b) Take her out shopping and buy something to signify her entry into womanhood. An article of clothing, a make-up case, a jewellery box, a hair-dryer or electric curling tongs.

c) Perhaps a 'Bat Mitzvah' or 'Welcome to Womanhood' party could be given. This would need to be associated with age and not with the starting of menstruation. The latter is a private happening which should be kept within the immediate family, though celebrated nevertheless.

The giving of a father's blessing

Children who can enjoy the presence of an available, loving father are fortunate indeed. In such a family a formal blessing pronounced by a father who has waited on God for inspiration is doubly blessed. There are many different settings in which this special blessing could be given.

a) Birthdays would be a good time to lay hands on and pray over your children.

b) Sunday lunch could be another special time when you could lay hands on each member of the family and bless them in turn. One man read Gary Smalley and John Trent's book *The Blessing* and took the idea so seriously that he began blessing his family at the evening meal. He would lay hands on his wife, pray a blessing on her, and then he would move to the children and pray a blessing on them.[1]

c) Praying a blessing upon each member of the family at a special New Year's Day celebration could be a wonderful way to start the new year.

d) But above all, a special blessing should be given when a son or daughter is about to leave home for another episode in their life, such as boarding school,

[1] McDowell and Wakefield, *The Dad Difference*, p. 107.

college, moving into their own flat or leaving home to get married.

e) Search the scriptures and mark the different blessings with which you could bless your family. The most famous is the blessing Aaron and his sons used to bless the Israelites: 'The Lord bless you and keep you; the Lord make his face shine upon you and be gracious to you; the Lord turn his face towards you and give you peace' (Num. 6:24–6).

Praying for the family

As we have suggested, a blessing which contains future predictions is only possible from a father who has spent time listening to, watching and praying for his children. How can a busy father find the time to pray in such a committed way for his family?

a) Use the time on the journey to and from work to pray for your family.

b) Take fifteen minutes out of your lunch break to pray for them.

c) Get up fifteen minutes earlier in the morning.

d) Ask God to speak to you prophetically about the family, i.) when you are reading the Bible, ii.) through dreams and visions, iii.) by drawing your attention to something special about your son or daughter.

For divorced or separated fathers

Even though you may no longer be living in the same house as your children, you are still vitally important to them. It will take more effort for you to keep in touch with them, but you need to do so through all the means open to you.

a) Write letters.

b) Send regular postcards.

c) Phone every week.

d) Visit regularly.

e) Where and when possible, have them to stay and take them on holidays with you.

f) Plan outings together, such as a museum which is of special interest to them.

g) Try to remember their birthdays and other special occasions such as the ones mentioned above.

h) Remember a father's special blessing is still yours to give.

i) Above all, don't involve the children in the difficulties you have had, and may still be having, with their mother.

j) Make sure they know that they were not to blame in any way for your separation.

Hints to mothers

It may be tempting to think that you are more important to your children than your husband is. Certainly in their infancy it may have appeared that way. It is true that your roles are distinct and the children need you both for different reasons. But your importance in their lives is equal. If the imbalance that exists in homes today is to be redressed, your help will be vital.

a) Believe that your husband has an important part to play in the home.

b) Encourage rather than bully him to play his part.

c) Don't protect your husband from the children, as if he was exempt from responsibility.

d) Give them the opportunity to work out their relationship.

e) Don't interrupt them when they spend time together, even if it gets heated.

f) Provided it is reasonable, allow your husband to discipline the children.

g) Be loyal to your husband in front of the children.

h) Don't criticise your husband in front of the children or behind his back.

i) In particular, beware of over-protecting your son(s). Encourage the men in the family to spend time together.

j) Praise your husband when he does a good job of fathering.

Suggestions for churches

The values of secular society have a tendency to infiltrate the Church and in today's world fathers are either ignored or marginalised. Churches could lead the way and give some practical help to change this situation.

a) Use Fathering Sunday to teach on fathering. Recently I was asked to address a 'men only' meeting on the subject of fathering. Although it was the first time such a meeting had been held in that particular town, nevertheless the hall was full. The men were interested enough to give up an evening. Afterwards many asked for prayer to become better fathers.

b) Father and son weekends/evenings could be organised by the church for those whose sons have reached the age of 'initiation' into manhood.

c) When the girls reach a similar age, an acknowledgement by the church could serve to prompt fathers in their job of affirming their daughters.

d) Men with young families should be encouraged to spend as many evenings at home as possible, instead of at meetings in the church.

e) The Sunday morning arrangements should be appropriate for all the family. The service should either be one in which the children can participate, or children's groups should be provided where the children are happily catered for. In this way families are encouraged to come to church together.

This is by no means an exhaustive list. You could even spend a family discussion time talking about what they would like you to do with them.

As you decide to put as much as you are able to into your family, physically, emotionally and spiritually, you will reap the benefits and later they, and their children, will rise up and call you blessed.

REVIEW FOR FATHERS

If a question is not appropriate to your children's age, answer the question as honestly as you can for the future (would) or the past (did).

Time

Yes No

- ☐ ☐ Do you attempt to spend time with each of your children?
- ☐ ☐ Do you help put them to bed?
- ☐ ☐ Do you read to them?
- ☐ ☐ Do you play games with them?
- ☐ ☐ Do you take them on outings they enjoy?
- ☐ ☐ Do you make sacrifices to be with them?
- ☐ ☐ Do you spend your leisure time with them?

Communication

Yes No

- ☐ ☐ Do you enjoy talking to your children?
- ☐ ☐ Do you enjoy listening to them?
- ☐ ☐ Do they tell you their troubles?
- ☐ ☐ Do they tell you when they are happy?
- ☐ ☐ Do you tell them you love them?
- ☐ ☐ Do you cuddle them?
- ☐ ☐ Do you encourage more than criticise them?
- ☐ ☐ Do you keep the promises you make to them?
- ☐ ☐ Can you tell when they are unhappy?

Educational

Yes No

- ☐ ☐ Do you make things for your children?
- ☐ ☐ Do you make things with them?
- ☐ ☐ Do you watch TV together?
- ☐ ☐ Do you teach them new skills?
- ☐ ☐ Do you help them with their homework?
- ☐ ☐ Do you explain to them the things they do not understand?
- ☐ ☐ Do you tell them about your work?
- ☐ ☐ Do you know their teacher?
- ☐ ☐ Do you attend the parents' evenings at their school?

Discipline

Yes No

- ☐ ☐ Do you discipline your children?
- ☐ ☐ Do you think of appropriate punishments?
- ☐ ☐ Do you make sure your relationship is restored before bedtime?

Affirmation and initiation

Yes No

- ☐ ☐ Would (did) you acknowledge your son's entry into manhood at puberty?
- ☐ ☐ Would (did) you celebrate it in some way?
- ☐ ☐ Are you a good model of masculinity for your sons?
- ☐ ☐ Would (did) you tell your daughter you were proud of her when she became a woman?
- ☐ ☐ Would (did) you celebrate this happening in some way?
- ☐ ☐ Are you appropriately affectionate with your children?
- ☐ ☐ Do you answer your children's questions about sex?

Spiritual

Yes No

☐	☐	Do you pray with your children?
☐	☐	Do you read the Bible with them?
☐	☐	Do you take them to church?
☐	☐	Do you share your faith with them?
☐	☐	Do they know you love Jesus?
☐	☐	Do you lead a family prayer time?
☐	☐	Do you pray with them when they are sick or have problems?
☐	☐	Do you make it a priority to answer their questions?
☐	☐	Do you bless your family on special occasions?
☐	☐	Do you pray regularly for your family?

A score of less than 23 answers in the affirmative would indicate some improvement was needed in your fathering skills.